POWERED BY
HOPE

POWERED BY HOPE

THE TERI GRIEGE STORY

Everyone has a cancer. Everyone has a dream.

Teri Griege
with Amy Marxkors

TWO HARBORS PRESS

Cover Design by Kati Griege
Typeset by Kristeen Ott
Photograph on front book cover by Nato Neri, Cinesthesia Productions

Printed in the United States of America

To God, Dave, Kyle, Kati,
and The Army

CONTENTS

FOREWORD

by Chrissie Wellington

I frequently close my eyes and recall the glorious sunrise on one Saturday in 2011. I visualize the ball of fire rising up over the volcano, bathing light on the Pacific Ocean and signaling the start of a day that would be like no other—a day that, when over, would change the lives of all those who stepped into those Pacific waters. To most it was a day like any other, but to the other 1,500 people standing shoulder to shoulder with me, that sunrise marked the dawn of hope. It marked the start of the Ironman World Championship.

Saturday, October 8th, 2011, was the day I embarked on one of the biggest endurance challenges in the world together with a woman who epitomizes what it means to be truly extraordinary. That woman was Teri Griege.

Ironman inspires like no other sport. It transforms the lives of those who take it on; and those who take it on transform, in turn, the lives of others through the heroism of their deeds. One of the beauties of triathlon is that professionals such as myself get to race on the same stage as the amateurs—sharing the smiles, the grimaces, the highs, the lows, the tears, and the joy—united by the same goal: to cross the World Championship finish line in Kona, Hawaii. We race together, suffer together, and celebrate together. And when one speaks of motivation, it is the recreational athletes who inspire me the most, and none more so than Teri.

Imagine battling and overcoming alcoholism as a young adult only to be told, years later, that you've been given a death sentence in the form of colon cancer. Imagine then being told that it has spread to your liver. Imagine enduring multiple rounds of radiation, debilitating chemotherapy, and invasive surgeries. Imagine then suffering from related infections and further physical and emotional setbacks. Imagine doing this whilst training for one of the most challenging endurance events in the world. Teri doesn't need to imagine. This is her story.

Teri has experienced more suffering, pain, discomfort, anguish, and disappointment than any of us could ever think possible: challenges that would have forced many to bow down and concede defeat. But instead of curling up and dying, she has fought these battles with the most powerful weapon of all: Hope.

In the words of Martin Luther King, Jr., "Everything that is done in the world is done by hope." To Teri, at times, hope was all she had. She dreamt of a time when she could be free of addiction, of a time when she could be given a clean bill of health, and of the time when she could cross the hallowed finish line at the Ironman World Championships. On that Saturday in 2011, with a body still wracked by stage IV cancer yet powered by courage, resilience, and unwavering hope, Teri realized her dream.

Since that seminal day I have had the privilege of getting to know Teri and am deeply honored to be able to call her a friend. Her triumphant story is a beacon of light for us all to follow: an inspirational reminder that extraordinary is not the province of cinematic superheroes, but of everyday people. Extraordinary is to pursue your passions, to overcome huge odds, to defy expectations, to look fear in the face and to achieve more than anyone would ever think possible. Extraordinary IS Teri Griege.

Of course, it is not only her amazing and awe-inspiring achievements that inspire and instill belief in all those around her, it is Teri's tireless and selfless devotion to helping others: racing for a cause that is bigger than herself and altruistically giving back to the world in so many ways.

Teri once told me, "I have two major goals: to inspire others and to save lives." Teri is achieving both, more successfully than she could ever know. Her amazing story is a beacon of hope: encouraging, guiding, and inspiring us all.

Smiles,
Chrissie Wellington
Four-time Ironman World Champion

A NOTE FROM TERI

Writing a note for the book *Powered By Hope* seems like a daunting task. Why? Because in my mind, heart, and soul there is so much I want to say and so many people I want to thank. How can I possibly remember to include everything and everyone? I can't.

Let's talk about the Everything—there are a few pivotal days that come to mind. The day Dave and I were married. The days I gave birth to Kyle and Kati. The day I committed to become clean and sober. And the day I was diagnosed with cancer. Each of these days were filled with gifts—yes, even the day I was diagnosed with cancer. Cancer has made me a better person, and for that I am grateful.

Let's talk about the Everyone—first to Dave, Kyle, and Kati. You are my heart, my reason, my powered by hope! I love you more than you will ever know. To my immediate family—Mom, Mimi, JoAnn, and the entire "Francisco" family—wow! How lucky am I to have all of you in my life? You lift me up. To Daddy and Ma—who I turn to in heaven— thanks for listening. To the Griege family—your strength and support, near and far, has always been felt. To the entire army—"Teri's Troops"—thank you for marching along on this journey with me. If you are reading this, please know that you have touched my heart, and I hope I have touched yours.

In many ways this feels like a crazy dream. Cancer, Kona, speaking, a book—this can't be me. I truly hope that the honesty in this book helps others. If just one person accepts his or her addiction or gets screened for cancer; if just one life is saved, this book will have served its purpose.

One final thank you—to Amy. Without your hard work, talent, and vision this book would not exist.

Love and Hugs to all.
Fueled By Faith and Powered By Hope,
Teri

A NOTE FROM AMY

The island looks small from the skies—even when the skies are navigated in a nanoscale prop plane that seats six passengers (allegedly). We—that is, the pilot, a quartet of locals, and I—landed at 9:31 p.m. Hawaii-Aleutian time. Dave and Teri were already at the airport, waiting for me behind a chainlink fence separating the tarmac from a small parking lot. They waved as I made my way down a wobbly set of aluminum stairs leading from a miniature door near the tail of the plane.

"Here is your lei!" Teri said, greeting me by placing a fragrant fuchsia and indigo flower strand around my neck. "You're in Hawaii now!"

We exchanged hugs as though we were old friends. In truth, we were relatively new acquaintances. I had met Teri two weeks before, at the Siteman Cancer Center, where I was interviewing her for a local article. The interview was initially supposed to take place over a quick, twenty-minute phone call.

"You know, I was thinking . . ." she had said when I called her, my cell phone set to speaker and propped up against a stack of books next to my laptop. "Why don't you come with me to my last chemo treatment before Kona? You can see what this cancer business is all about."

A few days later I was in the parking lot of Siteman.

"Teri?" I called to the younger of the two women walking with the easy confidence of routine toward the sliding glass doors across the way.

"Hey, Amy!" Teri replied. She introduced me to her sister Mimi before resuming her march. "You ready?"

Was I ready? For the interview, yes. But for the launch of a two-year adventure our impromptu date was about to occasion? Well, maybe not.

As I followed Teri from room to room, down long hallways, and through a welcoming committee of nurses; as I sat next to her in the treatment room while chemo pumped through her bloodstream; as I listened to her ask, with the familiarity of dear friends, each person who passed how the family was doing, how that new bike was working out, how Brady played in his last soccer game; as I listened to her nonchalant references to eighty-mile bike rides and twenty-mile runs, her gratefulness evident even in her modest deflection of praise; as I watched the graceful reconciliation of two bodies—an elite athlete and a cancer patient—in a single, exceptional person, I began to realize the story I was about to write would require much more than the allotted eight hundred words.

I will never forget that first night in Kona, when Teri and Dave momentarily abandoned all with which they should have been preoccupied—an army of family and friends converging on the island, obligations with NBC Ironman Productions, race-day logistics and preparations, and, of course, Teri's own health—to pick up a young, travel-weary writer whom they had just met. They greeted me with hugs, carried my bags, and escorted me back to their rental car, all the while asking how my trip had been, if my flights had been on time, if I had eaten anything, if I was hungry or thirsty or tired, if the tiny plane was, indeed, really as awful as it looked. Teri asked about my own marathon training; she asked about my parents. She told me the condo where I would be staying was very clean and very nice and decorated well. ("You know, you book these things online, so you never really know until you get there," she said, shaking her head.) The biggest race of her life was just days away, and yet she spoke nothing of herself.

That's the thing about extraordinary people: they rarely recognize their own heroism until after the fact. And most of the time, not even then.

Many people have done great things. They have scaled mountains, sailed across oceans, survived the wilderness, conquered nations, defeated armies, and walked on the moon. But extraordinary doesn't happen overnight. To climb Everest, we must first tackle the foothills. It is not a single act of greatness that elevates our character, nor is it a single obstacle that defeats us. For every shock-and-awe battle in life, there are a hundred wars of attrition. After all, it was but a straw that finally broke the camel's back, and death can come by a thousand cuts. There is something to this idea of countless trivial matters adding up to something great. Namely, every extraordinary feat is contingent on the nature of our ordinary actions.

We often use military terms to describe our relationship with cancer. We speak of fighting, of refusing to surrender, of battle and war, of courage and victory. But how do we apply these decorative figures of speech to an unglamorous reality? What does the application of the metaphor look like, say, in the life of a suburban mom?

It looks, in truth, very *daily*.

There are no bright lights or glitter in Ironman training. There is nothing romantic about colon cancer. And certainly there is nothing pleasant in combining the two. The whole affair is humbling. It is trying. It is tiresome. It is monotonous. It is uncomfortable. It is very, very difficult.

Yet as I sat there at Siteman, watching this attractive, vibrant woman embrace a situation that has no appealing merit of its own and transform it into a startling vision of beauty, athleticism, and grace, I was struck by the extraordinariness of her ordinary. Her everyday shattered the status quo and eliminated excuses. Her everyday was an act of rebellion against the expected. Her everyday gave hope.

Writing this book has been an incredible journey. Along the way, I have had the honor of meeting countless individuals without whose time, knowledge, generosity, and patience this book would not exist. To Teri's family I give my utmost gratitude: Dave, Kyle, Kati, Mimi, JoAnn, and Laverne. Thank you for letting me crash your vacations, parties, and meatloaf dinners. Thank you for putting up with my questions, being so open in your answers, and trusting me with your stories. To Teri's army, especially Jeff Eddy, Scott Stern, Ruben Aymerich, Cristel Santiago, Beth Zubal, and the nurses and doctors at the Siteman Cancer Center and Barnes-Jewish Hospital: thank you for giving your time, experience, insight, and expertise. To Michael Snell: thank you for your counsel, for believing in this project, and for representing us from the beginning.

And, of course, Teri. Thank you for allowing me the privilege to tell your story. You truly are extraordinary.

Sincerely,
Amy L. Marxkors

PROLOGUE

They say you can hear it for miles. It is a distant reverberation, a barely perceptible clamor that slowly separates itself from the softer sounds along Ali'i Drive. You hear it before you realize what it is, but as your weary legs carry you ever closer, you know. It swells in the darkness. It thrusts reality before you. It jars you into a consciousness you have methodically buried and denied over the course of 140.6 miles.

It is the finish.

The finish line at the Ironman World Championship in Kona, Hawaii, rivals Times Square on New Year's Eve. Ask anyone hovering within the neon glow of the lights and flapping banners and pulsating dance music and giant screen broadcasting the triumphant celebration as each of the eighteen hundred participants crosses the finish line—ask the athletes, the spectators, the volunteers, anyone. The energy intrinsic to an event designed to challenge the elite of the world's elite athletes to the ultimate test of physical endurance is overwhelming in and of itself. Add to that the unique trials suffered and victories celebrated by each athlete—both in the race and throughout training—and you have a finish line scripted for a blockbuster film.

Fourteen hours and fifty minutes after wading into Kailua Bay, a lean, tan woman with a giant smile and a blonde bob makes her way across the final hundred yards of the course. She takes her time, slapping high fives and sharing hugs with the hundreds of spectators lining the finish chute. She has suffered, and she has endured. She smiles. She laughs. She shouts in triumph. She soaks in every second of her glorious, bold, defiant act. But she doesn't hurry. Today—tonight—there is no need.

Yes, this race was slower than her other races. She has had a tough go of it over the past couple of years. Chemo has taken its toll on her body. So has the radiation. Surgery and infection have compromised her body's ability to recover. Her stamina isn't what it used to be. She has struggled to keep up her weight. Neuropathy has settled in her hands and feet. She knows this may be her last Ironman. But none of that matters. Teri's mission has nothing to do with time, nothing to do with pace, nothing to do with a personal record. Teri's mission is simply to complete the task at hand.

Teri's army, a motley crew of soldiers nearly three dozen strong, drafted by her diagnosis—their oaths of loyalty cemented by blood, business, and friendship—wait at the finish line. They know she is coming. They watch the clock, eagerly, anxiously, every moment expecting to see her athletic frame on the giant screen just beyond the finish line. The crowd continues its cheers as Mike Reilly, the patriarch of the Ironman finish line, anoints finishers with his hallowed benediction.

Finally, they see her.

"From St. Louis, Missouri . . . here she comes!" Mike cries above the din of music and ovation. "Currently being treated for stage IV colon cancer, raising two children, undergoing chemo . . . Teri Griege!"

Smiling, laughing, waving, she crosses the finish line. Her family has been given access to the finish area. Her husband, Dave. Her children, Kyle and Kati. Her sisters, Mimi, ever stalwart, and JoAnn, who is battling cancer herself. Her mom, the ageless Laverne. Dr. Ruben Aymerich, her gastroenterologist who had the painful duty of delivering the devastating diagnosis. And, of course, her soft-spoken oncologist, Dr. Ben Tan. They embrace her as she covers her face with her hands, tears flowing—easily, unreservedly. They are tears of joy, of relief, of knowing what lies ahead, and of not knowing.

"Let's do it again together, okay?" Mike prompts the rapturous crowd as Kyle places the lei around his mother's neck. "Together! Teri! You are . . . an Ironman!"

The cry is loud and impassioned. It is a collective blessing, the strength of thousands. Family. Friends. Strangers. They surround the finish area, their voices fused and synchronized in a single purpose. They are an army. They are one.

Ironman World Champion Chrissie Wellington, hours removed from her third-straight victory, throws her arms around Teri as the NBC cameras hover around the two and giant production lights swath them in a brilliant white glow. More tears. More words of congratulation. More words of hope. Finally, it is time to move on from the glitz and chaos of the finish line. Past the photographers. Past the giant glowing screen. Away from the music and the noise. Teri is led to the athlete's tent. She needs fluids and food. She needs to get warm. She disappears behind the giant scaffolding.

It is over.

For all of the trials encountered during an Ironman, they say the hard part isn't crossing the finish line. It's getting to the start.

For Teri, it was an odyssey that covered many years and many struggles, with challenges extending far beyond the miles. There was alcoholism. There was recovery. There was faith. And then there was cancer. But each trial served its purpose, and by the time the searing heat and belligerent winds came screaming across the black lava desert of Kona, she was ready.

When Teri was diagnosed with stage IV colon cancer, she didn't know it would provide a platform for a defiant declamation of hope. When she plopped her bag of chemo on a barstool next to her indoor bike trainer and cranked out two and three hours on the bike, she didn't know she was breaking all the rules. She didn't know she would inspire thousands of people or save hundreds of lives, her own sister's included. She didn't know she would form an army or that her story would be told across the world. She knew only that cancer wasn't going to stop her from training, from racing, from living. She never thought she was doing anything out of the ordinary. In her mind, she was simply doing what she had come to do.

But on that steamy October night, beneath the brilliant lights mounted on the giant scaffolding looming over the cheering crowds and reflecting atop the waters of Kailua Bay, as she crossed one of the most coveted finish lines in sports, she proved the exceptional. It was more than a race. It was a swashbuckling declaration of hope, a fourteen-hour victory lap across a scarred and volcanic landscape born of hidden turmoil, one that vividly represented her own baptism by fire, and it was written long before she toed the start line of her first triathlon, long before she was diagnosed with cancer, long before she ever dreamed of competing on the sacred soil of the Big Island.

POWERED BY
HOPE

1

BLONDE HAIR AND BUDWEISER

I was the baby of the family, and a surprise package, to say the least. I was the youngest of three girls. My sister Mimi was fourteen when I was born; JoAnn was thirteen. My sisters still remember the day our dad told them another sibling was on the way. He piled them into the car for a trip to the grocery store, and for a while, it was business as usual. But then he broke the news. Mom was going to have another baby. They thought he was joking.

As it turned out, Dad wasn't joking, and on July 17, 1961, I entered the world. The wide age gap created a unique dynamic between my older sisters and me. While I was toddling around and burbling my first words, Mimi and JoAnn were already full-fledged teenagers learning how to drive, going on dates, and preparing for college. In many cases, I was part of the process. They toted me around on shopping excursions and schlepped me to friends' houses and, during the summer, slathered me in sunscreen and lugged me to the pool. JoAnn started dating her future husband, Chuck, when she was just fourteen (he was a mature eighteen), and they would take me with them on dates to the store or the ice cream parlor. They were often complimented on their "darling baby." It was a fitting, though specious, assumption. I was everybody's baby. While JoAnn cooked dinner, Mimi would feed me, bathe me, dress me, brush my hair, trim my fingernails, hone my manners, and generally fuss and fret over me. JoAnn was the first to get married; she and Chuck moved to Columbia, Missouri, when I was still very young. Mimi stayed in St. Louis after she got married, and I was often dropped off to spend the day with her, always to the tune of "My Cherie Amour," which she sang to me constantly. And if my parents, Laverne and Dick, were going to be out for the evening—as they often were with my dad's job as a salesman in the railroad car business, they would drop me off at Grandma Ida's for the night, where I learned the finer points of gin rummy.

Grandma Ida and I shared a special bond. I was seven when Grandma Ida moved in with us. Grandma Ida lived with us for twenty-five years, and we grew very close. Once, when Grandma Ida and I were home alone, someone tried to break into the house. Grandma Ida heard the ruckus and began screaming, scaring the would-be intruder away. The whole affair proved to be rather traumatic for me, and from that point on, I refused to sleep anywhere but in Grandma

Ida's room. Grandma Ida and I were roommates for a solid three years.

Sports were a part of my life from an early age, even though no one else in my family was an athlete or even close to it. I was six when my mom enrolled me in dance class. I suffered through two years of tap dance and pirouettes before I finally hung up my dance shoes for the last time. Plus, I had discovered something I really enjoyed doing: swimming.

I was seven and all legs and arms. My parents signed me up for the swim team at Sunset Country Club. I won my first race and nearly every race after that. My father never missed a meet. He would pace up and down the pool deck, cheering my name and whistling loudly, two fingers in his mouth. He got a kick out of watching me swim.

I enjoyed other sports as well. I started playing "bitty basketball" when I was eight and tennis and golf when I was nine. In high school, I played field hockey and basketball (our team three-peated as state champions), but swimming was still my métier. I was the first swimmer from Visitation Academy to go to State. I did, however, earn a rather notorious distinction in field hockey. During practice one day, I fell and knocked out my two front teeth with the butt end of my stick. The school instituted mandatory mouth guards from that point on.

My husband, Dave, grew up on the fairways of Greenbriar Country Club. He was one of five children—four brothers and a sister. His dad, Charles Griege, was a prominent cardiologist, having founded the cardiology department at St. John's Mercy Hospital in St. Louis. Dave attended St. Louis Priory, an academically rigorous Catholic all-boys college preparatory school. The schedule at Priory was demanding, with school, sports, Mass, and homework filling the hours from early morning to late evening. There was little time for play. But when there was, Dave and his brothers spent it on the golf course.

Considering the notorious latticework of the St. Louis parochial school system and country clubs, it was no surprise that as kids Dave and I had heard of each other. What was surprising was that until the Fleur de Lis dance, we had never met.

Fleur de Lis dances were courtly affairs associated with pomp, circumstance, and the Catholic school system. It was the type of thing grandmothers love and young boys being trammeled by bowties and tuxedo jackets hate. Polished shoes. Long dresses. White gloves. A real *Leave It to Beaver* country club soirée. June and Ward would have approved. But Dave and I were sixteen, and neither of us wanted to be there.

Yes, we had both grown up on the monogrammed side of the tracks—tennis rackets and golf clubs in tow—but we had no use for the polished set. Life was more fun when you weren't always worried about a few scuffs here and there. Heck, life was the scuffs. And if one thing was for certain, it was that the quarterly Fleur de Lis dances were as finely shellacked and scuff-proof as any social gathering of high school students could get.

Straightjacketed by the quarterly observance, Dave made his way across the room and introduced himself. He asked me if I wanted to dance. I said yes. He was the first boy I danced with that night. He was the only boy I danced with that night. There was instant chemistry.

Our first real date was a sledding excursion with friends on Art Hill in Forest Park, a quintessential St. Louis winter activity. The scene is always extraordinarily picturesque. At the top of Art Hill sits the Art Museum, an imposing, white-columned building built for the 1904 World's Fair. Bowing deferentially to the museum is the hill itself, a spectacular grassy descent cascading from the Art Museum down to a small lake that rests below. A few inches of snow, and Art Hill is transformed into a Norman Rockwell with a palatial backdrop—sleds, scarves, mittens, and all.

To this merry milieu Dave and I headed. By the time we arrived, many of our friends were already speeding down the slope toward the lake below. Dave tossed his sled on the ground and motioned for me to join him. I climbed aboard, and away we went. This was more like it. Excitement. Adventure. Competition. And the occasional high-speed crash.

We dated the rest of our junior year, and even though by the time we were seniors we had started seeing other people, we shared the same social circles and often hung out. When graduation rolled around, Dave headed off to Dallas to study economics at Southern Methodist University; I made the two-hour trek from St. Louis to the University of Missouri. Communication became less frequent, curbed by the consuming distractions of increasing workloads, new schedules, and fresh social circles; but we never let negligence corrode our relationship. Every holiday, spring break, and summer, we would reach out to each other for a phone call or a visit. Still, the long distance took its toll, as it inevitably does. Our friendship remained strong, but the tangibles of our relationship became less apparent. Slowly, we faded from each other's everyday lives.

The setting of our first date was both symbolic and prescient. Dave and I, racing away from the pageantry and decorum looming above and into adventure. It was a thrilling ride not without bumps and dangers. We didn't know it then, but life would soon throw its own set of obstacles in our path, threatening all we knew and hoped for.

I started drinking in high school. At first, it wasn't anything excessive. Friends, parties, and alcohol went hand in hand in hand, and there was no shortage of the three. Dave and I never showed up to a party empty-handed. We always brought a six-pack of Budweiser and a cheap bottle of champagne. It was our trademark.

But even as a teenager, I began to crave the escape alcohol provided, temporary though it was. I liked the buzz it gave me. I drank when I wasn't at parties. I drank when I was alone. Beer. Hard liquor. It didn't matter.

And then came the pot. Someone brought a small stash of marijuana to a party. I was game. A few puffs. A few more. It could have passed for typical high school carousing, the aggregate of juvenile shenanigans, peer pressure, and teenage rebellion. But for me, it was more than that.

On the outside, I seemed to have it together, but I was secretly tormented by my own copybook image. I was the all-American girl, good at sports and school, hair coiffed and clothes perfectly pressed, down to the smallest fold of my deep burgundy pleated jumper (Grandma Ida and my mom made sure of that). But I was acutely aware of my own shortcomings, and I was held captive by the fear that my ideals and expectations were slipping through my fingers. It wasn't one big thing. It was a mountain of small, seemingly negligible pressures and insecurities. Plus, I simply liked the feeling of being high and buzzed. When I wasn't, reality was too—real. I'd sit on the back patio and wonder why I felt the way I did. Why I felt a void. Why I felt depressed. I had everything I could want. It just didn't make sense.

So, I'd take a drag. Or I'd drink. It was immature—I knew it—but it was also self-medicating. And soon I was irreversibly addicted to my own destructive prescription.

The transition to college life at Mizzou was silently traumatic and contributed to my addictions. At eighteen, I was just as much the incorrigible homebody as I had been when I was eight—probably more so. When I was little, I would go to sleepovers only to call my parents in the middle of the night, homesick, begging them to come pick me up. Even when I would stay at JoAnn and Chuck's for the weekend, my mom would have to talk me down from a metaphorical ledge and cajole me to brave the night with my sister. I hated being away from home. Home was my security blanket. My dad had insisted I go to school at Mizzou for exactly that reason. It was only a couple of hours away, he reasoned, and JoAnn and Chuck lived right there in Columbia. I could visit my sister if I started to feel homesick.

When I revealed I wanted to study health and physical education, my dad suggested I go to business school instead. Business, he said, is a broad and relevant field of study. I wanted to be a gym teacher, but I thought perhaps my dad knew better than I did. I thought perhaps I was wrong and should set my sights higher than a high school gymnasium. And, really, Columbia wasn't that far from St. Louis. I could still visit home on the weekends and hang with JoAnn during the week.

I decided to go to Mizzou, but I wasn't happy. I was confused. I felt pressured. Away at college, I drank even more.

It was easy to drink—a lot—without anyone noticing. People were always going to bars. Someone was always having a party. Most of the time I'd start drinking on my own before heading out, just to take the edge off. Getting marijuana wasn't an issue either. Down the hall in my dorm were several girls who smoked pot religiously. I joined them. Often. Daily. It was convenient and easy and anesthetizing. It was a flawed system, and I knew it; but it was like a light switch in my body simply flipped on. And so I drank. And I smoked. And the downward spiral began.

Soon my major didn't matter. Getting into business school—or any school—was no longer an option. My addictions affected my studying. For the first time in my life, my grades plummeted. It was a discomfiting turn of events. I had always excelled in school. I had always played sports. I had always overachieved. My identity hinged on the approval of my parents and teachers and coaches, and I had worked tirelessly to appease them. In high school, my drinking problem had been somewhat curbed by the compulsion to please. But at Mizzou, where I no longer played sports, where academics existed with greater autonomy, and where I was surrounded by unbounded opportunity to indulge my habits, the tenuous harness was removed. In the process, my one source of fulfillment—shallow though it had been—was lost. I filled the void with more drinking. I studied less. My grades fell. I felt guilty. I drank more. It was a vicious cycle.

It was 1979. I had been away at school for one month.

By the time my sophomore year rolled around, I was frightened enough by my own addictions that I told my parents about my struggles. My mom asked if JoAnn and Chuck would let me live with them while I went to school. They immediately created a little apartment for me in their basement. For several months, I lived in relative, albeit temporary, restraint. I drank less frequently than I did when I was in the dorms; and when I did drink, I was careful never to return to JoAnn's house hammered. My dalliance with moderation gave me a false sense of control. Toward the end of the semester, I moved back to the sorority house on campus. But my addictions immediately returned, more consuming than ever. It was a miserable existence.

Just before Christmas break of my sophomore year, I approached my parents again. I needed help. My conscience was the one thing that saved me. I knew something wasn't right. I knew I needed help. I just didn't know what to do about it. I didn't know who to turn to. Addiction is a vicious circle. You medicate your feelings. Then you realize that something isn't right. Then you feel guilty. You medicate some more. It's awful.

My parents placed me at Highland Center, a thirty-day inpatient rehabilitation program in south St. Louis. A greeting room on the main floor separated two wings. The first wing was for new residents undergoing detoxification, a process that usually takes several days, though the time and method of detoxification varies greatly depending on the drugs being flushed from the patient's system. The second wing was for the rehabilitation programs: individual therapy sessions, lectures, group therapy, and counseling.

My time at Highland Center was tough. The schedule at Highland Center was tight and monotonous, and there were very few young people at the facility. Most of the patients were middle-aged and in a completely different stage of life than I was. There was no one I could relate to. No one to cling to. I was away from home, away from my friends, away from the life I had known. I was very, very lonely.

After completing one month at Highland, I returned to my parents' house. I never went back to Mizzou. There was too much temptation and not enough accountability. Instead,

I applied for nursing school at Missouri Baptist Hospital in St. Louis. It was a year-round program. I could live at home, go to school, and move forward with my life.

Two and a half years later, I was a registered nurse. I moved out of my parents' house, bought a condo in Brentwood, and got a job at a small branch hospital in the fiercely quaint community of Kirkwood. I still went to Alcoholics Anonymous meetings, though as the pieces of my life fell into place and my confidence grew, I attended less frequently. I was healthy. I had an apartment. I had a job. And I had just reunited with Dave.

We bumped into each other at the grocery store and discovered that, in a twist of fate too wild to chalk up to mere coincidence, Dave had purchased a condo in the same complex as I had. Here we were, after being apart for four years, living only a few doors down from each other. We played catch up. Dave had graduated from SMU with a degree in economics and was immersed in the world of mortgage banking. I talked about my new job at St. Joseph's in Kirkwood. Dave already knew bits and pieces about my drinking problem, but the details were hazy. And I certainly wasn't in any hurry to explain them.

Dave's dad, Dr. Charles Griege, had been a mainstay during my time at nursing school. While attending classes at Missouri Baptist Hospital, I had secured a part-time job at St. John's Mercy Hospital where Dr. Griege headed up the cardiology department. Occasionally, I'd run into him. We would always take the time to chat. We were fond of each other. Throughout my junior and senior years, when Dave and I would pile into our friends' cars and pop in and out of the Griege household, Dr. Griege's stern, dark features would always soften into a smile when he saw me.

It was with a heavy heart, then, that I listened to Dave's news. Dr. Griege, the stalwart patriarch, had passed away earlier that year, in July. He died of leukemia. I knew he had been sick—I had talked to Dave once or twice early in the summer, and he had given me updates—but I didn't know the cancer had finally run its course. Dr. Griege had been larger than life, a pillar of strength in his family and his community. He was a physician, a friend, a husband, and a father. His patients adored him. His friends loved him. His family cherished him. He was admired and respected not just for what he did, which was considerable, but for who he was. It was an irrecoverable loss. Dave mourned his father deeply and silently.

Dave and I picked up where we had left off in high school, as friends more than sweethearts. Dave had been a notorious serial dater at SMU. (A fact to which Dave's brother Mark paid tribute in his toast at our wedding rehearsal dinner. "Teri," he said to me, hoisting a scroll of computer printer paper in the air, "here is a list of all the people Dave has dated." He then unfurled the scroll, which fell across the table and onto the floor.) And yet, for all of his prolificacy in the dating world, Dave never had a steady girlfriend. I had also dated off and on over the years, but neither of us was in a relationship by the time we reunited at Brentwood Forest. So, we hung out with each other. We talked on the phone, watched TV, and shared sodas. The magnetism between us was matched only by the ease and familiarity that characterized our relationship. Several months after our chance meeting at the grocery store, we realized we should probably start dating each other again. And so we did.

It was an up-for-anything, live-for-the-fun-of-it relationship, cemented in both undeniable attraction—the

one we had known nearly seven years earlier at the Fleur de
Lis dance—and the easy familiarity of best friends. Both
athletically inclined, Dave and I enjoyed the city's bountiful
sports scene. We spent many summer evenings downtown
under the arches of the old Busch Stadium, cheering on the St.
Louis Cardinals. Dave played softball, and we would hang out
with his teammates for post-game drinks at O.B. Clark's, an
infamously smoky Irish corner bar just a block from where we
lived. When the weather was nice, we'd grab our rackets and
hit the tennis courts at John Burroughs High School before
heading down the street to Hunan Wok, where we would
always order two large servings of cashew chicken.

Coordinating our schedules wasn't easy. I often
worked the graveyard shift at the hospital, starting my workday
as Dave was ending his. Even my dayshifts clashed with Dave's
eight-to-six schedule. But we made it work. I would stop by
Dave's condo before heading to my own for the night, even if
for only a short visit. Dave would be falling asleep on the couch
when I'd knock on the door and wake him up. We would sit
together and watch *The Tonight Show* or sports highlights and
fill each other in on the day's adventures. Sometimes we'd talk
for an hour. Other times it would be thirty minutes. But we
always made time.

The real fun was on Friday and Saturday nights, when
we would gallivant down the streets of the Central West End,
an eclectic cradle of art and culture where hipsters and the
well-to-do cross paths with stone-broke college students.
Tom's Bar and Grill was a favorite for burgers and fries;
Balaban's for drinks and live music. The latter, which served
fine Italian fare, was too pricey for us, so we would often
toss a frozen pizza in the oven or stop by Steak 'n Shake on

our way out. Then we'd spend the evening strolling the tree-lined streets of Euclid Avenue, peering through the hubbub and clatter of sidewalk cafes and restaurants in search of familiar faces. In the days before smart phones revolutionized communication with virtually unlimited accessibility, Euclid Avenue was the connection line.

It was soon obvious to everyone—including us—that we were meant to be together. That we would get married was as certain as the cashew chicken at Hunan Wok. There was only one hiccup. After two years of serious dating, Dave still hadn't proposed.

To his credit, he had gone as far as purchasing a ring, though the question remained unasked. By August of 1986, my patience had deteriorated to dangerously low levels. What is he thinking? I wondered. Are we ever going to make something of our relationship? Well, if he thinks I'm just gonna wait around forever, he is wrong.

Dave nearly cost himself a sheepish trip back to the jewelry store when he left for a weekend in Dallas to visit his brothers Mark and Chuck. Dave had made the trip to tell his brothers that he was going to ask me to marry him. But he never made me privy to this rather critical detail, and I found the timing of Dave's vacation exasperating. Certainly, I thought, if he were going to propose, he would have done so by now. Yet Dave returned from Texas tightlipped. Needless to say, I wasn't thrilled.

The following weekend, Dave planned a Cardinals baseball outing with our good friends, Dave and Kathy Diemer. Dave had remained close friends with Diemer throughout college, and we reunited in St. Louis, making many of our excursions double dates.

Dave told me the day's plan. We could spend the afternoon together and meet up with the Diemers in time for the Cardinals game. I agreed, but Dave wasn't off the hook. I was still piqued by Dave's silence regarding the small matter of whether or not we were going to spend the rest of our lives together, as opposed to just an afternoon.

As we did on many weekends, Dave and I hit up the tennis courts at John Burroughs. During the drive to Burroughs, Dave baited his questions with hints to the imminent proposal. He had been baiting me all week, but I wanted nothing to do with an inquisition.

"So," he asked as he drove, "if you were going to go on a honeymoon, where would you want to go?"

I was not amused.

"Don't mess with me, Dave," I said.

He just smiled. Quiet ensued.

By the time we stepped onto the hard courts at Burroughs, I was in no mood for chitchat, and what ensued was a tennis match for the ages—or at least for the grandkids. I drilled groundstroke after groundstroke in frustration, each of my shots aimed directly at Dave's head. I was so mad. Dave knew I was riled up and decided that two could play that game. He returned my salvo with a battery of crosscourt shots, running me from one sideline to the other and back again. The more I ran, the more frustrated I became, and the more I tried to pound the ball down the court and, ideally, down Dave's esophagus. We both emerged from the final set unscathed, though there wasn't much conversation on the way back to our condos. Dave dropped me off at my place and headed to his own to shower and get ready for the evening. If there was an evening, that is. At that point, I wasn't certain I would even go to the baseball game.

An hour later, Dave knocked on my door.

"Let's go," I said unceremoniously, letting him in.

"How 'bout we sit on the couch for a bit and talk."

"No."

"C'mon. Let's sit for a while. Just a little bit."

"No."

"C'mon, Ter."

"No.

Finally, however, Dave won out. I shuffled my way to the couch. Dave sat down, facing me. I turned my back to him.

"Ter . . ."

Nothing.

"Ter."

Arms folded.

"I really do love you."

Nothing.

"And I really do want to be with you."

Still nothing.

"And I really want to marry you."

He held out the ring box, though the motion went unnoticed since my face was still turned in the other direction.

"If you're playing another game with me, Dave Griege, I'll . . . I'll . . . I just can't take it anymore!"

I turned around, faced flushed with both exasperation and hope. He was looking at me, his arm still extended. I looked down at the small package in his hand.

"Just open the damn box."

A diamond ring was nestled inside.

I reached for the phone to start spreading the news. Dave, however, nixed my broadcast plans. He had one more trick up his sleeve, and it involved our closest friends and family.

"You can call anybody you want tomorrow," he said, "but now we're going to the game. Then we'll come straight back here—just the two of us."

Thirty minutes later, Dave and Kathy Diemer appeared at the door. Dave had made them privy to his plan, and they arrived with the deliberate sureness and telltale grins of those included in a small circle of confidence. Hugs and congratulations abounded as I showed off my ring and chronicled the day's events, including my previous desire to leave a "Wilson" tennis ball logo imprinted on Dave's forehead.

"Wait," Dave called, halting the group as we headed out. "There's only one rule tonight: We're just going to the game—just the game. I know we're going to see a bunch of people, but we're not gonna go out and party." He looked at me. "Tonight is just about us."

As it turned out, Busch Stadium that night was an assembly hall for our friends. I showed everyone my ring as we bumped into people we knew. Amidst the cackling admiration were countless invitations to celebrate.

"C'mon! Let's go out!"

"Let's meet up after the game! Drinks are on us!"

It would be fun. Everyone wanted to go out.

"Nope," Dave said. "You made a deal with me. Tonight is going to be special. Just us."

We turned down the invitations, explaining that we were going to spend a quiet evening together. After the game, the Diemers brought us back to my condo.

"Why don't you guys come up and have drinks with us before you go?" I asked.

"Oh, no, no."

"Are you sure?"

They were. The Diemers smiled and said goodbye.

The stairway leading up to my condo was famously dark, and every time Dave and I returned from an outing, I'd purse my lips together and make an "ooo-EE-oo" sound—like *The Twilight Zone.*

This time was no different, and as I "ooo-EE-oo-ed" my way up the stairs, it was all Dave could manage not to laugh. He knew what awaited me at the top. He also knew that what—or, more accurately, who—awaited me could no doubt hear my comical call. I opened the door and flipped on the light. The entire room was filled with friends and family.

"Surprise!" they cried in unison.

I was stunned and started laughing. There was a smorgasbord of guests—my parents, Laverne and Dick; Dave's mom, Dolores; JoAnn and Mimi; my nieces, Christi, Courtney, Julie, and Cary; Dave's brother Jeff; our closest friends. And food. Lots of food. (Mimi made sure there was enough to feed an army.) We celebrated and ate to our hearts' content, which was reached sometime after 1:00 a.m.

Anyone peering through the window of my Brentwood Forest condominium at the faces inside—happy, smiling, content—would have come to the conclusion that things were finally right in my life. I had my ring, my degree, a good job, my own place, a close circle of friends, and the love of my life. From the outside looking in, life was good.

But surfaces can be deceiving. Yes, the tenuous exterior that had begun to crack while I was in high school and that had shattered at Mizzou had been repaired, and the broken pieces neatly swept under the rug. The shell had been restored. I, however, had not. My insecurities remained. As did my fears. I was twenty-five years old. Many of my friends were already married, already had kids, already had a fine, two-story brick home in West County. It was all very picturesque, very expected, very much where I thought I should be. I was engaged, which was a step in the right direction; but still, I felt behind the curve. Wasn't I supposed to be leading the way? The pressure, guilt, and anxiety was as claustrophobic as it was self-imposed.

My time at Highland had served as a punctuation mark in my life, but it hadn't started a new chapter. It was a pause that momentarily halted the negative momentum. The Alcoholics Anonymous meetings were the most helpful. Through the program's Twelve Steps, which centered on admission, forgiveness, and restitution, I was able to acknowledge my issues and take practical, calculated steps to circumvent the addiction cycle.

But the principles of AA tackled the addiction, not necessarily the reasons behind it. In some ways, the Twelve Steps were another form of medication. A healthier form of medication? Yes. But as anyone who has ever plucked weeds from a sidewalk crack can tell you, unless the root is removed, the unwanted vegetation will grow back—often stronger for the pruning. Roots are persistent that way.

For me, the steps of AA were a supplement to a core restoration that had yet to take place. The shell that had been repaired was just that: a shell. There was still a void. And nature abhors a vacuum.

2

REHAB, RELAPSES AND RECOVERY

I was at a party. Dave was there. It had been almost five years since my time at Highland. Five years since I had had my last drink. And life was good. Life was normal. I took a mental inventory of my situation and came to the conclusion that I finally had control of things. I looked around at my friends. They were chatting, laughing, sharing drinks, and happy. After years of peppering my conversation with gracious refusals of drink offers, I decided I was ready to rejoin the milieu of social libations. I figured I'd give it a whirl.

I ordered a beer. I had two that evening. The earth didn't crumble. The skies didn't fall. No big deal. It was fine. I was fine.

Looking back, I realize that normal drinkers probably don't want a beer at four in the afternoon. But at that time, I convinced myself it wasn't that big of a deal to drink a beer in the middle of the day. I figured if I played my beer card at four, then I just wouldn't drink anything the rest of the evening. I thought I could do a kind of "controlled drinking." I was wrong.

The principles expounded in Alcoholics Anonymous helped me keep my addiction in check, but they couldn't resolve the heart of the issue. Spiritual though not religious in nature, the Twelve Steps revolve around admission of one's addiction and accountability to self, God, and others. In the AA program, recovering alcoholics make "a decision to turn our will and our lives over to the care of God" and trust a higher "Power" to help them. To maintain inclusiveness of all faiths—or lack thereof—references to God are tagged with the qualifier, "as we understand him."

While fair enough, the intentional ambiguity saddles a vital part of the healing and recovery process on a person's understanding of God. This can pose a problem if someone's idea of the divine is fashioned after parental or authority figures with less than desirable qualities: apathy, incompetence, vindictiveness, pettiness, narcissism. Then, of course, there is the God often propounded by religion, the deistic over-seer who cares not so much for the individual as he does for ceremony and ritual. A God so petulant and fallibly human doesn't provide much comfort to someone in the throes of struggle and addiction.

My concept of God wasn't enough. To me, God was inseparable from institutional Catholicism—formal prayers, cryptic rites, and perfunctory attendance. Obey the rules or be damned. My religion consisted of the occasional foxhole prayer. To me, faith wasn't relational. It wasn't personal. It wasn't spiritual. It was all about image.

Yet despite my understanding of God as sterile and apathetic, I knew there was something more, something I was missing. There was this hole in my life—unidentified, unrecognized—that left me unsettled and discontent.

I had experienced the "something more" once, in high school. I went to a weekend retreat through TEC—or Teens Encounter Christ—a Catholic organization that puts on a series of weekend retreats for high school students. I went with a friend from Visitation, a popular girl who partied even harder than I did. I still don't know why we went or what could have convinced us to waste a precious weekend on a spiritual retreat. But I do know why I didn't obstinately refuse: as cool as I thought I was and as impervious as I appeared to others, there was a part of me that knew there was something else out there. I had no idea what it was, where it was, or how I was supposed to get there; I knew only that it was there and that I wanted it desperately.

A prominent feature of TEC retreats is the involvement of those who have attended in previous years. TEC graduates write letters to current participants, encouraging them in their faith and acting as personal prayer warriors. Some of it seemed a bit gimmicky to me ("I will put pebbles in my shoes so that every time I take a step, I will think of you and say a prayer," one letter read), and I wasn't sure I bought into the whole Jesus thing. Still, I was intrigued.

At the end of the retreat, the senders and receivers of the letters met for the first time. The students linked hands and were led to a dark gym, where they formed a ring around the perimeter of the basketball court. Then, the lights were flipped on, illuminating a new group of students standing in the center of the circle. The letter-writers, in the flesh.

I remember standing there, looking at the smiling faces of the total strangers who had been praying for me the entire weekend. Whatever they had was real. They truly believed it. They acted on their faith. They were loved by something—Someone—bigger, and in turn, they were able to love, even complete strangers.

My heart had been touched at TEC, but it hadn't been pierced. My experience at the retreat intensified my conviction that there was something else without prompting me to take active steps to find it. My search was in the passive tense. I didn't want to seek as much as I wanted to be found.

Now, standing at the bar with my friends, I was no closer to fulfillment than I had been over a decade before. The seeming stability I had achieved over the past years was tenuous, and the two beers I had that evening created an invisible fracture in an already suspect foundation.

It was a slow, silent splintering. At first, it was simply social drinking, controlled and unremarkable. At parties. With friends. At sporting events. No one suspected anything. On rare occasions, I'd have a drink or two too many. But that was an anomaly, not the norm. On the outside, I held it together. On the inside, I was empty.

It was a six-year regression. I stopped attending AA meetings once I started drinking again. I couldn't face my group knowing I was drinking between classes. With sly and stealthy steps, my addiction returned. I would have a drink before I headed out to the bar or to hang out with friends. I would drink late in the afternoon, before Dave got home. I'd drink after I got home from work. I also started smoking pot again. It was harder to get, but when I could get my hands on a stash, I'd smoke it until it was gone. It was a closet addiction, one I hid well. I looked forward to the weekends when I could let loose and not worry about broadcasting my secret to the world. Drinking on the weekends was normal. If I got a little crazy, who cared? It's what people did. No one would give it a second thought. And no one did.

The weeks and months passed and quietly slipped into years. Dave and I got married. A few months later, we moved from our condo in Brentwood Forest to our first home, a two-story, red brick house with green shutters. It was a quiet neighborhood with tree-lined streets, a perfect place to start a family. I had Kyle. I had Kati. It was all very West County and very much the mirror image of what I had feared would never happen. The veneer looked better than ever, shiny and smooth and tinted with all the right domestic hues. And yet, the ache only worsened, as did my addictions. I knew there was more. I wanted more. But I couldn't find it, so I self-medicated. I couldn't find relief in any other manner. There was just a hole.

I was a roller coaster of insecurity. Some days I felt one up on the world—smart, athletic, and accomplished. On other days I felt incurably inferior. I'd look in the mirror and see only someone who was unattractive, incapable, and amateurish. The constant rises and falls of corkscrew comparisons created an emotionally dizzying environment. The horizon was forever changing, my mood forever shifting. It was exhausting. I'd stop drinking for a while because I was disgusted with my alcoholism. Then I'd drink again because I was depressed. Then for a while I'd be fine. Then I would be depressed again. It was like I had motion sickness, and I swallowed my addictions like Dramamine.

In 1991, I approached Dave. He had known something was wrong, but he hadn't known the extent of my relapse. I told him it wasn't good. I told him I needed help.

I enrolled at Edgewood, a thirty-day inpatient program at St. John's, similar to Highland. Again I fulfilled my obligations in recovery. I attended group therapy and private counseling, lectures and AA meetings. I went through the motions, completed the program, and headed home.

I relapsed within two weeks.

I longed to break the cycle, but I didn't know how. I used the tools I had gathered at rehab to chip away at my addiction, desperate to keep things under control. But one can whittle only so long before the arms grow tired. Within a month, both of my addictions returned, stronger for the attack. I was trapped in a Sisyphean battle, and I knew it. But a silent, persistent voice—I think it was my conscience, which never fully surrendered—compelled me to keep fighting.

I knew I was losing the war, but I wasn't going to go down without a battle. I rejoined AA and quit drinking after the first meeting. At first, the temptation to drink was overwhelming, but eventually the hourly battle became daily, and then even weekly. I was what AA terms a "dry drunk," someone who doesn't drink, but still exhibits the same emotional instability and behaviors as an alcoholic. (AA reserves the designation of sobriety for those who both abstain from alcohol and are mentally and emotionally healthy.) Interim periods of sobriety peppered the next eighteen months. I wasn't perfect, but I did the best I could. My existence was that of a sick person trying to get well. Some days I felt strong. Some days I didn't.

But in December of 1992, I relapsed for a third time. Dave had had enough. He gave me an ultimatum. My secret habits weren't going to find asylum under our roof any longer. I could have my addictions or I could have a home. But I couldn't have both.

In short, he kicked me out. And in the process, he saved my life.

*　*　*

JoAnn woke up to the sound of frantic knocking. It was late. Close to midnight. Maybe later. She stumbled out of bed and made her way through the darkened hallways to the front door. Flipping on the porch light, she saw a slumped and shaking figure in the soft, yellow glow.

I had made the drive from St. Louis earlier in the evening, but spent hours wandering around Columbia before I finally—and incredibly, considering my condition—made my way to JoAnn's. Like Dave, my family had given me an ultimatum. They were done. They loved me, but they weren't going to let me flush my life down the toilet. It was the simple application of tough love, a final resort for a family watching the systematic self-destruction of wife, mother, daughter, and baby sister.

What that meant, exactly, I didn't know, nor did I know the parameters of my banishment. As I stood on JoAnn's front porch, I wondered if she would take me in. I had nowhere else to go. Even if I had, I would have been physically unable to do so. It was a miracle I had made it to JoAnn's in the first place. And so, broken and sobbing, I knocked on the door and waited. The action itself was a splinter of hope. It was admission that I needed help.

JoAnn opened the door as I fell into her arms. My clothes were disheveled and dirty, my hair a mess, my face stained and swollen with tears and the grime of travel. I was drunk. And high. JoAnn wrapped her arms around me and carried me inside.

Not sure if I was simply coming off a high or on the brink of cardiac arrest, JoAnn monitored my every breath, word, and action. I was beside myself with grief and anger and remorse. Like a mother caring for her young child, JoAnn got me out of my bedraggled clothes, gave me a shower, and draped me in a fresh pair of pajamas. I was still crying as JoAnn put me in bed. She stroked my hair and spoke quietly. Several hours passed. Finally, I fell asleep. Holding vigil as she sat on the edge of the mattress, JoAnn made sure my trembling had fully succumbed to slumber before she headed to her own bed.

Sleep never came for JoAnn, but for me, it did, serving as a literal and figurative tidal wave washing away the physical chaos of the night before. I woke up the next morning with my head cleared and my vision restored. I knew what I wanted. And I knew what it would take to get there.

That morning, JoAnn called a friend whose husband was a counselor. He made arrangements for us to visit a rehab center in Fulton, Missouri, not far from Columbia. We met with an advisor who escorted us around the building, showing us the center and explaining the rehabilitation program. The center, however, was full, and I couldn't be admitted.

I stayed with JoAnn for three days before heading back to St. Louis. During that time, we went on long walks and talked for hours on end. My emotions and hopes spilled forth in a way they never had before. I wanted to be clean, yes, for myself, but above all for my family. That's what I wanted more than anything else. I wanted my family again. I wanted to be a strong and loving wife to Dave. I wanted to be a nurturing mother and pillar of strength for Kyle and Kati. I wanted the four of us to love each other and need each other and spend time together and live free of my addictions. Ultimately, it was my love for my family—for Dave, Kyle, and Kati—that propelled me to seek healing.

I returned to St. Louis, heading not to my own home, but to Mimi's. I visited several rehab centers around the city—Christian Northwest, St. John's, St. Anthony's—to see what help was available. Christian Northwest had an outpatient relapse prevention program, and I figured it was worth a shot. For two weeks, I made the daily drive to North St. Louis County. But the program was limited by its outpatient format and, not inconspicuously, its focus on cocaine addicts. Needless to say, I didn't match the environment. At the end of the second week, one of the physicians at the facility pulled me aside.

"Look," he said, his voice growing somber, "if you want to survive, you need to go into long-term treatment."

He directed me to Parkside, a recovery center in the suburbs of Chicago. He had gone there himself. The center ran a specialized program for people in positions of public influence and responsibility—such as pilots, doctors, and nurses—for whom addiction bore serious professional consequences. As a nurse, I fell into that category. As a repeat offender, I needed something more intense than a thirty-day outpatient program. Parkside catered to both of my needs. To Parkside I would go.

I returned to Mimi's house and gathered up the few items that I would bring with me to rehab. Then I called Dave.

The conversation was pragmatic and unemotional. I told him I would be at Parkside for three months.

Mimi took me to the airport the next day. I set my bag on the concrete curb separating the drop-off point from the bag check just outside the main terminal. We hugged and said our goodbyes. Mimi drove away while I made my way through security and down the long, low corridors leading to my gate. It was a forty-five minute flight from St. Louis to Chicago. A staff member from Parkside was there to greet me at O'Hare when I landed. We shook hands, made quick introductions, and hopped in a car to head to the recovery center. Finally, I was getting help.

Parkside Recovery Center operated on juxtaposition. Fitted together like the intertwined fingers of a clasp were personal autonomy and vital partnerships with others. The marriage of these two elements formed the foundation on which the program's philosophy hinged. Unlike at Highland, where patients had rooms inside the main building, at Parkside, patients stayed in off-site apartment complexes. It was the individual's responsibility to attend classes, lectures, group therapy sessions, and AA meetings. Meals were also the patients' responsibility—and a primary vehicle connecting independence and communal living. Residents at Parkside stayed in two-bedroom apartments, four people per unit. Each apartment was issued a weekly food voucher. Residents had to make group excursions to the grocery store and agree on what was purchased. Transportation also fused self-reliance with reliance on others. Getting to class was the responsibility of the individual, but because many patients arrived without a car (I fell into this category), the four-mile trek to the main building often mandated asking fellow residents for a ride. It was an exercise in assistance—seeking, receiving, and giving. And because getting to treatment required effort, Parkside effectively made recovery a choice. Patients could choose to get better, or they could choose not to. What was not open to question was learning how to survive in a temporary family forged by shared trial and nine hundred square feet of living space.

Even in one's own apartment diversity abounded. When the only common factor threading its way through a conglomerate of individuals is the relatively multifarious one of alcohol or drug addiction (or both), eccentricities are bound to flourish. My apartment was no different. There I was, the west St. Louis County prep school product with the hair, clothes, and comportment to fit the bill. And there was Laura, Tif, and Suzy.

Laura was my roommate. A nurse, wife, Mormon, and mother of three, Laura had wiry blonde hair and over-sized eyeglasses. Her clothes were simple. Her appearance, however, belied the rather scandalous nature of her private life. Just before arriving at Parkside, Laura had gotten herself arrested at Walgreen's after she helped herself to her doctor's DEA number and tried to pick up a forged prescription.

On the other end of the social spectrum was Tif, an attractive, sporty, Southern beauty with wavy brown hair, perpetually tan skin, and wide, flirty eyes. In simple terms, Tif was all about Tif. She had always been popular and was used to being the center of attention. She had no desire for Parkside to be any different and quickly established herself as the treatment center's luminary.

But once again, appearances were deceiving. Tif, the beauty queen whom the boys adored and the girls envied, was secretly bisexual. Her own closet sexuality existed paradoxically with her job as a therapist for children who had been sexually abused. In the latter identity she encouraged the open expression of deep wounds; in the former, she concealed her own.

Rounding out the quartet was Suzy, an attractive Southern woman with chic Dionne Warwick hair and a polished mien to match. Academic and intelligent, Suzy was a pediatrician whose cavalier, adventuresome disposition lent an especial empathy to her occupation.

Considering the smorgasbord of personalities crammed into our small little apartment, relative peace reigned. Hubris is quickly smothered by shared living spaces, food vouchers, and vehicles, and camaraderie is accelerated by the simple desire to maintain sanity. Three months is a long time for close quarters, previously acquainted or not. Plus, the underlying reason for our stay at Parkside united us in a very real, very sincere way.

In the outside world, all four of us lived in masquerade. No one suspected the subservient Mormon housewife wore a façade as simply and unassumingly as she wore her plain clothes and quiet tone. No one realized the flirty, Southern beauty queen was smothering her lonely secret beneath crowds of worshipers, or that the doctor who deftly healed children and offered words of reassurance to worried parents was herself incapable of crying out for help. And if you had looked at me from the outside, you would have thought I had everything imaginable—my appearance, my marriage, my house, my children, my faith, my workout regimen. But as the saying goes, you can't judge a book by its cover.

All four of us had the outside world fooled, but at Parkside, bluffs were called. It's tough checking yourself into rehab and then trying to convince fellow patients that you've got everything under control. At rehab, it's house rules, and if you want to stay in the game, you have to play by them, no matter who you are or pretend to be. There is a certain amount of vulnerability assumed when you admit your need for help and then actively seek it. And what we did have in common— addiction, humility, awareness, a desire to get well—out-weighed our differences tenfold.

Take Harold, for example.

Harold was a powerline repairman for an electric company. He had a Fu Manchu and long, salt-and-pepper gray hair that he combed back to his shoulders. He wore jeans and cowboy boots and a black leather vest with fringed edges. He didn't talk much. When he wasn't repairing high-voltage powerlines, he was riding his Harley. And every August, he trekked across the country to the Sturgis Motor-cycle Rally in South Dakota, the largest, raunchiest biker festival in the world, where nearly half a million leather-clad bikers transform the town with its two bars and a bowling alley into a seven-day lollapalooza of bikers, beards, and bikinis, complete with a machine gun firing range, drinks at One-Eyed Jack's Saloon, and souvenirs at Renegade Classics Rally Gear. Harold was perfectly at ease in the midst of the raucous ruckus of Sturgis and remained faithful to his annual pilgrimage even after he became sober, an impressive feat when you consider the rally drowns itself in overcrowded bars and giant banners advertising the refreshments within.

But it was at Parkside, in a small group therapy session, that Harold and I met. The rough-hewn tattooed biker sat down next to me. The day's session required each participant to prepare a short biography and then read it for the class. One by one, we revealed our separate roads to addiction. I read my story. And then Harold read his.

His father had disappeared when Harold was only a few years old, leaving him, his young mother, and his sister to fend for themselves. One day, while the tiny family was still coping with the pain and trials of being abandoned, Harold's mother took her two children to the beach for a picnic. The swimsuited pair ran off to splash in the waves and build sandcastles, and when they returned to where their mother had set up camp, they found nothing but a small blanket and a few stranded toys. She was gone. They never found her. The weight of the world and of being a single mom had proven too much, and so she brought them to the beach and left them. Harold was six. His sister was eight.

Some fellow beachgoers found the two children crying, abandoned. Harold and his sister were placed in foster care, where they were eventually adopted by different families and shipped to separate states. They reunited decades later as adults, but the sibling bond had been irreparably severed. They were never close.

Harold's life seemed bent on a downward spiral from the beginning, and for many years it descended unfettered. But finally, alcoholism proved too much even for the gruff, Fu Manchu-ed lineman. He checked himself into Parkside Rehabilitation Center and ended up in small group therapy, sitting next to me.

Seemingly, we had nothing in common. But perhaps it was exactly because we hailed from different worlds that our friendship worked. Not only was there no compulsion to impress, there was no medium for it. Our respective games were on different playing surfaces and the scoring systems didn't translate. The only thing we shared was an enemy. We were fighting a common war, regardless of how we had arrived at the battlefield. And friendships are forged in the trenches.

Harold and I remained friends even after Parkside. He would call us every Christmas morning to see what Santa had left under the tree for Kyle and Kati. And every year, he would stop by our house on his way home from Sturgis. Looping his way through St. Louis, he'd show up unannounced and wait on the back porch until I came home from running errands or taxiing the kids around town. Harold was quite a visual surprise to a pair of unsuspecting eyes, a monochromatic apparition that clashed with the vivid greens and rosebud reds of suburban landscaping. Most people can't claim dual aesthetic assimilation in the worlds of country club couture and that of outlaw motorcycle gangs like Hell's Angels. Neither could Harold. His black leather garb, tattooed skin, and abundance of gray hair were about as compatible with his surroundings as my golf shirt and khaki shorts would have been at Sturgis. I always worried that one of our neighbors would call the police before I got home to let him in.

Fortunately, no one ever called the cops on Harold, and he remained free to spend the evening with us. He always brought Kyle and Kati motorcycle T-shirts from Sturgis, and the presentation of these gifts was a highlight of his visits. He still didn't talk much, even in the sanctuary of friends. He'd gladly offer the minimum number of words necessary to answer questions (or to make the occasional inquiry), but most of the time he'd just sit back and watch our happy quartet in the inevitable domestic scrambling and chaos of a young family. Then he'd hop on his Harley and ride away, disappearing until he returned—punctual to the season and abrupt to the day.

Harold's visits continued until 2001, when he was diagnosed with throat cancer. His condition was terminal. He called me and told me he was dying, but that everything— his will, belongings, paperwork, funeral arrangements—had been taken care of. Harold had no close family or friends, and he knew that I worried about him. I had brought up the topic once before. If anything were to happen to him, were his affairs in order? Now he could say that they were. He had met a woman at an AA meeting six months before his diagnosis, and they had fallen in love. I could hear the boyish delight in his voice, even as my own heart broke with the news of his illness.

Several months later, I got another call, this one from one of Harold's biker buddies. Harold was not doing well. He was in the ICU at a hospital in Chicago, and his condition was declining rapidly. I hopped on a plane and made the trip up to see him. By the time I got there, he had already had a tracheotomy, and a long tube protruded from his throat. I sat down by his bed. We chatted—he silently, scribbling his thoughts and jokes and sentiments on lined paper.

A few weeks after my visit, and less than a year after his initial diagnosis, Harold passed away. Once his condition had deteriorated beyond the point of hope, the doctors sent him home. Content in the peace of his own bed and the comfort of the woman he cherished, he was no longer alone. His greatest joy was that he had a loving girlfriend to whom he could give all of his earthly posses- sions, and that's exactly what he did. Harold, the little boy who had been abandoned twice and whose life path had taken him to the darkest recesses of addiction and isolation, died sober, happy, and in love.

Several times throughout my stay at Parkside, I returned to St. Louis for short visits. Sometimes I stayed a couple of days. On my last visit home before I was discharged, I stayed for a full week, testing the waters of daily married living before returning for good. Then it was back to St. Louis to give life—real life—another go.

Rehab had been a humbling experience, but it had also been freeing. For all the anxiety exposure causes, there is relief in being found out. It's a tiring act, that of constantly being on stage. Never able to let your guard down, you live in fear of a momentary slip that will cause your meticulously crafted world of lies to shatter, leaving you exposed and naked, without an identity. For me, rehab marked the release of a very heavy burden. It also marked the beginning of acceptance—acceptance of myself, acceptance of my struggles, and acceptance of something else entirely incompatible with my life before Parkside.

3

LIVING SOBER, FINDING GOD

L ake Geneva sits in the southwest corner of Milwaukee, Wisconsin. It is expansive and pristine and fringed by stately summer homes with sprawling back porches and gazeboed landscapes. At one point it was called "The Newport of the West" because it served as a haven for both the famous and the infamous, with names like William Tecumseh Sherman, Al Capone, Axl Rose, George Lucas, and Hugh Hefner (just to name a few) gracing its eclectic guest list. Because of its storied past, you could call Lake Geneva a lot of things. Ritzy. Peaceful. Flashy. Serene. A landmark. What you probably wouldn't call it is "spiritual." Unless, of course, you happen to have had a spiritual experience in its bucolic vistas. Then perhaps you would.

Of the many vessels bobbing up and down on the tempered waves of Lake Geneva, one belonged to a fifty-something, slightly balding dentist who also happened to be a resident at Parkside. He didn't have much hair, but he had a speedboat, and about six weeks into treatment, he invited Tif and me to the lake for a weekend. We were halfway through our stay at rehab, the point at which the joy of reaching the turnaround point competes with the rather killjoy fact of still having just as far to go. The trip would be a mental and emotional respite from the confines of city living. We were game.

It was a two-hour drive from Parkside to the lake. Tif drove while I sat in the passenger seat, enjoying the scenery. We chatted for a while, but soon the small talk gave way to silence, and there was just the wind and the trees and the sky. And then, it happened. A feeling came over me; there was clarity in everything I looked at. If I looked at a leaf, it was like I could see all the veins and workings that were in the leaf. Just by driving by. I could see everything. Suddenly, I could understand how I could live on the other side, how I could live in sobriety. I never really knew how I was going to do it before; now I had the confidence that I could. It wasn't a specific answer. It was simply, "You are going to be okay. It is going to be okay. I am going to take care of you." Over and over.

It was an utter and consuming sense of assurance, a fullness of peace. The wind. The lake. The colors. So vibrant. So real. I could feel them. It was a phenomenon unlike anything else I had ever experienced. It was a taste of the divine. A taste of the supernatural. A taste of a power higher than my own. It was the proverbial mountaintop experience, one that usually comes in mere glimpses. This time, it lasted three days.

I went for a run when I got back to my apartment at Parkside. I was consumed by a hyperawareness of the world around me. I felt peace. I felt joy. No, not the temporary emotion of happiness, but joy. The kind of deep assurance that remains even in the midst of devastating circumstances. The feeling was startling and proved a spiritual awakening for me, an epiphany of both the physical and the supernatural. For the first twelve years after I left Mizzou, I never accepted I was an alcoholic. Did I admit I was an alcoholic? Yes. Did I accept it? No. Admitting it is just sitting there and saying the words, but accepting it is embracing it.

Lake Geneva was my turning point. That was the first time I really accepted my disease. For the first time, I really believed in my heart that everything was going to be okay. I had faith. I turned my life over to God. I didn't know Christ at that point, but my heart and my spirit were being softened.

But a process is still a process, and such things take time. After my departure from Parkside in 1993 to 2006, I leaned primarily on the 12 Steps to help me deal with life after alcohol. Alcoholics Anonymous has a sponsor system that pairs a newer member with someone who has been in the recovery program for a longer period of time. There is no hierarchy system in AA, no coterie of staff with long trains of acronymed psychology or counseling degrees from leading universities. Instead, AA sponsorship hinges on the real-life experience of fellow recover-ees and the peer-to-peer trust that encourages the open, candid discussion so vital to healing.

I spoke often with my sponsor, Kate. Together we walked through the business of self-forgiveness. It was relieving not to bottle everything up anymore. It was relieving to talk to someone about my struggles and fears and insecurities. Slowly, the pieces came together.

I had self-confidence after leaving treatment. A lot of my insecurities were lifted, and I began working through others. There were times when I grew and times when I went backwards. But I figured I was doing something right, because I stayed sober.

It took a long time for me to forgive myself for what I had done in the past. Many, many years. Many prayers. Self-forgiveness didn't come in a moment or a day. It was a process. But once forgiveness began to sink in, all the guilt and shame was lifted—at least, a deeper level of it was lifted. I realized I couldn't keep making my sin greater than God. And I couldn't make my standard of forgiveness greater than God's.

Thirteen years passed after I left Parkside. Recovery and relationships and family melded into the simple ins and outs of daily life. Kyle and Kati grew up and hurtled through the milestones of childhood. Kyle followed in the footsteps of his dad, attending school at Priory and playing golf at Greenbriar Country Club. In fact, from the moment he was old enough to take actual footsteps, Kyle began playing sports. Basketball, baseball, football, golf, tennis, swimming—everything. Kyle's first set of golf clubs came in the form of a rainbow-colored Fisher Price collection when he was two years old. He'd run around the house, practicing his swing, using anything and everything as a golf ball. Once, when Dave and I were out to dinner, Kyle had a particularly boisterous round, and a bright blue driver ended up in the dining room chandelier. (Aunt

Kathy was left to clean up the mess before we got home.) But the practice paid off. Kyle played golf for Priory all four years of high school, acting as captain in his senior year, when his team won the state championship.

Kati, on the other hand, balanced sports with art. When she wasn't playing soccer, volleyball, softball, or tennis, she was molding chunks of clay at the pottery wheel or firing ceramics in a kiln or transforming a blank canvas by way of charcoal. Our house was the meeting place for Kati and her high school friends, and while Kati would be upstairs drying her hair, I would hang with the girls in the kitchen, chatting with them about life and grilling them about their plans for the evening.

Kati was still a toddler while Kyle was in grade school. I would pick up Kyle from school at St. Monica's, and we would spend the afternoons together, Kati in tow. Our favorite destination was Lix Frozen Custard on Olive Boulevard. Kyle would order a cookie dough concrete with double cookie dough. I would order an Oreo concrete with double Oreo. Every time. When Girl Scout cookie season rolled around, Kati and I would split an entire sleeve of Thin Mints. Daily. And when Dave was away on business trips, I'd pick up a cookie cake for breakfast. After all, when the father's away, the children will play.

The most infamous addition to our home was Sunny, a boisterous golden retriever with severe hip dysplasia, an insatiable desire for retrieving tennis balls, and frequent bouts of epilepsy. We had recently given away our German shepherd (he was a bit aggressive), and Kyle and Kati were devastated. They begged us for another dog. Dave and I weren't so hot on the idea.

"Well, we're probably not going to get another dog right now," I told them. "But why don't you do some research on adopting a dog. Like a stray rescue."

I agreed to take Kyle and Kati to the Kirkwood town festival where the local stray rescue organization would have a booth. We arrived at the festival and headed straight to the stray rescue table. An hour later, research presented itself in the form of a four-legged fuzzball named Sunny.

"How are things over there?" Dave asked on the phone later that night. He was in Scotland on a golf trip and didn't know about the new addition to our family.

Bark! Bark! Bark!

"Oh, uh, fine! Fine!" I answered, motioning with my hand to Kati to do something about Sunny, who was making a valiant—and ultimately successful—attempt from the basement to introduce himself to Dave.

Bark! Bark! Bark!

"That barking I hear better not mean we now have a dog."

I don't remember how the conversation went after that.

Between his occasional seizures and cornucopia of daily pills, Sunny wreaked havoc at our home. Earlier that year, Kati earned the distinction of having sold the most Girl Scout cookies in her troop. She must have sold at least two hundred boxes. My SUV was packed to the brim with Thin Mints, Samoas, Do-Si-Dos, and Tagalongs when Sunny discovered he had a sweet tooth—and that I had left the trunk open. Kati and I returned to the garage only to find Sunny in the car, buried under a pile of crumbs, chocolate, and mangled cardboard.

Then there was the time he ate five whole, raw chicken breasts that I had left on the counter to defrost while I was at work. We rushed him to the vet. Sunny ended up being just fine. He may have been epileptic, but he had a stomach of steel.

Eventually, Sunny had to be put down. The seizure medicine had ruined his liver and kidneys. Kati wrote a poem about him. She doesn't quite remember how it goes, but she knows it said something about his blue eyes, which is curious, since Sunny didn't have blue eyes. He did, however, match the drapes in the family room.

One summer I became particularly ambitious and tried to institute "Magic Mondays." Greenbriar Country Club was closed on Mondays, so with golf and swimming out of the equation, I decided we'd dedicate the day to culture and education. I bought a book filled with things to do in St. Louis, and every Monday I'd dress up the kids and drag them to museums and aquariums and other fine cultural institutions, filling their heads with educational facts along the way. Magic Mondays lasted one summer. They were a disaster. But I was trying.

And then there was the question of faith. I knew there was more. I had seen it. I had felt it. But I didn't have it. Perhaps that's why I struggled. Voids are painful. They are empty. They are the opposite of life.

Plus, I had questions. Kati's confirmation at St. Monica's coincided with the revelation of the widespread sexual abuse permeating the Catholic Church. I wasn't religious, and whatever remaining devotion to Catholicism I still harbored was subsequently shattered. It was impossible to reconcile the claims of church leaders with the reality of what was happening behind church doors.

I struggled with the idea of going to church. To me, church was boring—more ritual and routine than anything else. It was something I did because I was supposed to do it. Church wasn't a spiritual experience for me. It was simply keeping up appearances.

Shouldn't you want to go to church? I wondered. What is "church" anyway? And God. Who is He? It wasn't sacrilegious rhetoric. It was a genuine question. Surely I was missing something. Surely there was more to God than religion. Because, quite frankly, religion—at least the religion I had experienced—wasn't fulfilling. So what had I felt at the TEC retreat in high school? On the drive back from Lake Geneva? In the first days after my return to Parkside?

I had come a long way since then, emotionally, physically, and even spiritually. I had been sober now for over thirteen years. My marriage was stronger than ever. I was fitter and healthier than ever. I was happier than ever.

But still, there were the questions. And they nagged at me relentlessly.

Kati's confirmation proved to be a watershed. I finally acknowledged my doubts and decided to do something about them. What "doing something" meant, exactly, I didn't know. As it turned out, I didn't have to.

In the biblical book of Ezekiel, the eponymous prophet finds himself standing in a desert. Everywhere he looks, there is nothing but desolation and barrenness, except for one disturbing phenomenon. The valley is covered with dry human bones, scorched from the sun and scattered across the sand. The LORD leads Ezekiel back and forth among the bones before commanding him to prophesy to the bones and foretell a series of miraculous events. Ezekiel obeys unquestioningly.

> "Dry bones," he says, "hear the word of the
> LORD! This is what the Sovereign Lord says
> to these bones: 'I will make breath enter you,
> and you will come to life. I will attach tendons
> to you and make flesh come upon you and
> cover you with skin; I will put breath in you,
> and you will come to life. Then you will know
> that I am the LORD.'"

It is a gutsy way to address a desert full of calcium deposits. But his faith is well founded. The bones begin shaking in their shallow graves, and there is a great din of rattling and clamor as they begin taking shape as human skeletons. Tendons appear, securing the bones together. The newly formed infrastructures are covered with flesh, giving the appearance of humanity. The LORD commands Ezekiel to speak one more time, this time prophesying to the final transformation.

> "So I prophesied as he commanded me, and
> breath entered them; they came to life and
> stood up on their feet—a vast army."

The dry bones of my own spiritual life were being covered in flesh. The pastoral forests of Lake Geneva had been an unlikely catalyst, but the scattered pieces of my life were slowly coming together. And like the breath that emanated from the four corners of the earth, the prompts to take action—to rise to my feet, so to speak—materialized suddenly and from unexpected sources just as my questions about God and faith were reaching a crescendo.

The first came at the gym. One of the instructors had started going to a church down in Chesterfield Valley, The Crossing. I had never heard of it. But the girl at the gym really liked it. The second came a few days later, this time at the salon. My hair stylist had just started attending a new church—The Crossing. The following week, Dave and I were at dinner with some friends. The conversation somehow found its way to the topic of churches. Our friends had visited several different churches across the area, but they really liked the one they had visited that Sunday—The Crossing.

It was too coincidental to be—well—a coincidence. Not only did the same church keep resurfacing, but the consensus was unanimous: Everyone who went there liked going there. I was intrigued.

I brought Kati with me the first time I visited. We were a few minutes late (true to form), and through the doors to the sanctuary we could hear the worship music already in progress: the low reverberation of the drums, the clapping hands of the congregation, the peak of the refrain. A woman greeted us in the lobby, led us through the closed doors, and guided us through the dim lights and raised hands to our seats. The music ended shortly after, and the pastor began his message. I remember the message resonated with me right away. It spoke of something real.

For six months, I continued to attend services at The Crossing. I was surprised by an immediate connection to the messages I heard and the people I met. As it turned out, the 12 Steps from AA were based on the Bible. Furthermore, one of the very first services I attended opened with a testimony given by a young man who had struggled with a drug problem. Instead of aloof ceremony, I found real people—imperfect and transparent.

But there was something else, the crux upon which everything I heard and saw hinged: a resolute emphasis on the saving grace of Christ. The whole concept of God's love—that the Creator of the Universe would send His Son to die on a cross for my sins—was a concept too great for me to comprehend. I had always struggled with self-forgiveness. Now this divine grace offered an absolution much greater than my own from an Authority much greater than myself.

In a sermon around Christmas in 2009, the pastor talked about waking up spiritually, and how everyone wakes up differently to God and to belief. He made an analogy using alarm clocks and waking up in the morning. Some people set their alarms for 7:00 a.m., and they immediately wake up, jump out of bed, and go about their day. Other people have to set their alarms for 6:30 a.m. because they'll hit the snooze button over and over. But even though they are slower to wake up, they still wake up. That message was very reassuring to me because mine was a very subtle awakening.

The Crossing offered several different classes for further study in addition to the services. I joined one of the church's LABs (Learning and Belonging Group). LABs were for anyone who wanted to learn more about faith and meet others who also had questions. Once a week, I met with a small group of women to discuss that week's sermon. There was no homework and no pressure. You simply downloaded the questions, thought them through, and then showed up to class. If you wanted to participate in the class discussion, you did. If you didn't want to, you didn't. Eventually, Dave started going to church with me. For the first time ever, he had seen me looking forward to church. He had his doubts, but the change in me was significant enough that he figured he'd check it out.

Together we took a class called Explorations, a six-week workshop that covered the foundations of the Christian faith. As it turned out, one of the Explorations group leaders worked with one of my good friends from high school, Carrie. We had gotten into all kinds of trouble together back in the day. Carrie couldn't believe that I was attending church. By choice even. Soon after, Carrie gave Windsor a try. I guess she figured if I was going, well then, maybe church people weren't so weird after all.

Finally, I had found it. The "something more." It wasn't dead religion. It was a real, living, dynamic relationship with God. There was no more hitting snooze. The Explorations course was the final alarm in my awakening.

In Hebrew, it is called *ruach*—or "breath, spirit"—and it was the difference between a mess of assembled skeletons on a desert floor and the vast, marching army in Ezekiel. *Ruach* is the opposite of dead religion. *Ruach* is life.

On November 20th, 2007, I met with Judy West, one of the pastors at Windsor. It was mid-afternoon, and the bright light of winter streamed uninhibited through the giant glass windows. It was the kind of light that makes you squint despite an overcast sky, the kind of light that surprises you with its detail. The large space with its vaulted ceilings and contemporary design, usually bustling with church members running late and welcoming each other with greetings and hugs, was empty and quiet.

Judy and I sat on a low bench placed against a wall. We didn't talk long, maybe twenty or thirty minutes. I asked questions. Judy answered. It was honest and unadorned conversation. There was no music, no keyboardist playing slow chords as soundtrack punctuation to an evangelist's entreaty; no raised hands or closed eyes; no call to the altar; no emotional appeal or pressure from the devout masses. The setting was, in many ways, a reflection of the conversation itself. Quiet, exposed, and illuminated. It was there that I accepted Christ as my Savior.

On the wall across from where we sat praying was a giant cross. Made up of hundreds of broken tiles, each piece was a nexus put in place by someone who had entered into a personal relationship with Christ. Judy asked me if I wanted to add a tile to the cross. I was skeptical. This wasn't my cup of tea. Emailing Judy had been a big deal. Meeting up with her had been unprecedented. Talking to her about fear, faith, life and death, and eternal life—that was unfathomable. And now I was supposed to march up a flight of stairs and stick a jagged piece of tile to a giant, roughshod cross adorning the wall of some non-denominational, evangelical church? What in the world had happened to me? Who was I?

Judy went with me. Step by step, tile in hand, I made my way up the stairs. When we reached the top, I wrote a note on a small piece of paper. I glued it to the tile, added more glue, and pressed the tile against the wall. There. I had done it. It was real. Permanent.

Well, almost.

Judy and I weren't even halfway down the stairs when I heard a slight whooshing sound—like the sound of a small object brushing against a wall—and then a tiny plunk! The noises were barely perceptible. Judy didn't notice them. I did. And I knew exactly what had happened.

I could almost hear God saying to me, "Teri, you heard that tile fall off the wall. Are you gonna do something about it?" It was like God wanted to see if I was really going to go through with this. Sometimes I feel like I have to work twice as hard as I should to get somewhere. Sometimes I'm a slow learner. But the tile falling off the wall was like God's way of saying that I was in the right spot. I was doing the right thing. And He wanted me to be resolute in my decision.

"Judy," I said, "that tile just fell off the wall. We need to go get it."

I grabbed the tile, went back upstairs, and re-glued it. (But I picked a different spot the second time.)

Looking back at the progression of my faith, I see it was more of a helical journey that spiraled upward than a vertical rocket shot. I believed in a God, but it took years for me to accept him. I wanted His help—but I didn't know how to express my need for His help or how to get it.

In Chicago my faith became more spiritual. At The Crossing, it became relational. It became personal. That doesn't mean that on some days I don't tend to pull back in and try to take control. It doesn't mean I'm perfect—or even good—at any of this. But character defects are like that game Whack-A-Mole. They pop up, and you have to keep hitting them back down. I'm better at managing them now. It's a daily reprieve. It's a process.

4

THE LURE OF THE MILES

It started innocently enough. Such things usually do. It was the summer of 2002. I was in the middle of a three-mile jog on the treadmill when my niece Christi let herself in through the back door.

"Ter?" she called, making her way downstairs and peering into the workout area.

"Ye-ah? Oh, hey, Christi!"

We chatted about our day, our kids, and what we had going on that week.

"So I think I'm gonna run the Chicago Marathon," Christi said after a few minutes. She had already signed up for the race and was in the middle of training.

"Really?"

"Really."

"And you're training and everything?"

"Yeah. Someone told me to get Hal Higdon's book. Said it was a good training schedule to use. My next long run is ten miles."

"Yeah?"

"Yeah."

"You think you can actually do it?"

"Yep."

Do people really run that far? I wondered. I had never run more than four miles. The whole concept of running 26.2 miles was mindboggling. It wasn't that I was opposed to the idea; the thought simply had never crossed my mind. After all, 26.2 miles was a far cry from the two or three miles I'd been logging—and even that only sporadically. Back at Brentwood Forest, I'd go for an occasional two-mile jog. After Dave and I moved to our first home, I would venture to the track or a fitness trail at a local middle school. And sometimes I ran the paved walking path owned by St. Luke's Hospital. That pretty much summed up my running history.

Later that night, I told Dave about Christi's crazy marathon idea.

"She asked me to train with her, but I said no. I don't think I'm gonna do it."

"Why not? You're already running multiple times a week. You know you can run. You should do it."

Dave's confidence and encouragement stirred up the competitive nature in me. Plus, Christi was twelve years younger than I was. Added incentive. If she can do it, I can do it, I thought.

"Okay. Maybe I will."

It was mid-July. The race was in October. I told myself that if I could go as far as Christi was scheduled to that weekend—ten miles—I would sign up for the Chicago Marathon. I picked the walking trail at St. Luke's Hospital for my run. The asphalt path is roughly a quarter of a mile long and speckled with nurses and silver-haired senior citizens. Ten miles at roughly a quarter mile per loop equaled forty laps of the meandering walking path. Armed with a pair of soccer shorts and a cotton T-shirt—I didn't know anything about bringing water or consuming energy gels or pacing myself with a watch—I set out on my mission, clueless as to whether or not I could actually complete the distance.

Forty laps and countless nurses and geriatrics later, I did. I would run the Chicago Marathon.

Christi and I began training together. If not quite haphazard, our training plan was methodically sketchy. I invested in Hal Higdon's book, and we followed the beginner's program. We did our long runs together on the weekends. We still had no idea about proper hydration; I don't think I even started drinking water until mile eighteen. The night before our long runs, I'd throw a couple of water bottles in the car and drive the route, hiding the bottles at strategic locations along the course. It was something, at least.

We often ran on Olive Boulevard. There was a Kenyan runner who passed us every time we were out there. We felt like we were good runners because we were out there with him. We thought we were so cool. I'm pretty sure we thought we were as fast as he was. Okay . . . maybe not quite that fast.

Even though my training was casual, good ol' Hal knew what he was talking about. I was more than prepared on race day. I crossed the finish line in four hours, twenty-eight minutes.

Chicago had been a good life experience. I felt a sense of accomplishment in completing not only the race, but also the training. I felt I had earned my medal. And despite my post-race inability to descend anything resembling a staircase, I had even had fun. But I wasn't necessarily hooked. A marathon every couple of years or so was plenty. So I thought.

In 2004, I ran the Lewis and Clark Marathon, a flat, pragmatic course through St. Charles, Missouri. The race served as my endurance fix, for the time being anyway. For me, working out was about variety. The primary goal was not to get bored. I joined Club Fitness down the street and became a regular at Body Pump, a one-hour group weight-training class. After a few months of Body Pump, I thought it would be a good idea to bounce my way through some aerobics classes. Then I tried spinning. And at some point, I decided to give triathlon a whirl.

In preparation for Chicago, I had done my homework. In preparation for my first triathlon, a sprint distance tri at a local recreation complex, I did not. I signed up on a whim. I knew nothing about triathlon training or racing, and my first tri would be baptism by fire. I borrowed Kyle's old ten-speed bike and took it for short jaunts on the Katy Trail, a 240-mile crushed limestone drag strip that runs flat as a pancake along the Missouri River. Occasionally, I'd go for a run. I never swam until I jumped into the water on race day.

On race morning, I showed up at the St. Peter's Rec Plex arrayed in a black, one-piece, fashion swimsuit and toting a gym bag with some shorts, a T-shirt, and running shoes. I secured Kyle's bike on the bike rack, threw my stuff in a locker in the women's bathroom, grabbed my goggles and swim cap, and made my way to the pool deck.

I did just fine in the water. Out of the water . . . not so much. The other athletes around me raced to the transition area, ripping off their swim caps and goggles as they ran, their sole aim to lose as little time as possible between the water and the bike leg of the race. As the name implies, the transition area is a designated area through which all athletes filter as they make their way from one discipline to the next. All athletes, that is, except for me. Oblivious to the rush of participants around me, I hopped out of the water, flung off my goggles, and marched straight to the women's bathroom to change. I changed in complete solitude. I couldn't figure out where all the other women were. I had never heard of the transition area.

And there was the bike. Besieged by sleek riders on even sleeker road bikes, I pedaled Kyle's deep red, ten-speed mountain clunker in a twenty-one-mile exercise of futility. The time cushion I had built in the pool was subsequently lost in the bathroom and on the bike course. My T-shirt and baggy shorts snapped in the wind as I pedaled a bike three times as heavy as the bikes around me. I was such a pitiful sight, everyone felt compelled to cheer me on. They kept yelling, "C'mon! You can do it!" I looked so ridiculous. And then the seat broke.

I was a third of the way into the bike course—maybe—when the adjustable seat post gave way and dropped to its lowest setting. Suddenly, I found myself riding a bike while in a modified fetal position, my knees up to my chin, my arms straight out in front of me clutching the handlebars. The disadvantage of riding a mountain bike was now dwarfed by the disadvantage of riding a mountain bike while facing the very real possibility of taking a knee to the face. But I was determined. I continued pedaling and wobbling down the road. Then I remembered. I had a towel.

During my training for the Chicago Marathon, I had been introduced to the rather uncouth habits of distance runners. Namely, their broad definition of appropriate places to relieve themselves. With the convenience of unlimited bathroom locations without the concomitant convenience of actual bathrooms, I had adopted the habit of carrying emergency "toilet paper" in the form of a rag stuffed in the waistband of my shorts. I even cut slits in the towel in case the urge to go struck me more than once on a single run. This time, I used the whole towel, but not for sanitary purposes. I pulled to the side of the road and hopped off the bike. As the other participants whizzed past me, I began the deconstruction of the mutinous equipment. Off came the bike seat. Out came the towel. I jammed the torn rag as far down into the seat post as I could before replacing the seat. It wasn't a perfect method, but for Kyle's bike, it would have to do. At least now the seat was higher and I was no longer in any great danger of breaking my nose with my kneecap.

Clothes flapping, seat wobbling, knees slightly more bent than they should have been and incriminating pieces of towel peeking through the seat post, I finished the ride. It was twenty-one miles of conspicuity.

The run was uneventful and far more comfortable than the bike. Training for the Chicago Marathon had taught me what I needed to know about picking up one foot and putting it in front of the other. Two hours, twenty-eight minutes after jumping into chlorinated waters of the St. Peter's

Rec-Plex pool, I crossed the finish line. It hadn't been pretty or easy or quick, but it had been fun (relatively speaking) and, at the very least, unconventional.

I was very, very proud of the race numbers tattooed in permanent marker on my arm and leg. I went straight from the race to Greenbriar to celebrate Father's Day with Dave and the kids. I ate lunch at the pool and kept my numbers on the whole time. I didn't want to wash them off. The numbers weren't battle scars, but they were like a membership card. I had joined the triathlon club.

Still, a sprint distance triathlon is a far cry from an Ironman, and I had no intention of pursuing the sport further or to such extremes. The sprint tri was the end of it.

The "end of it" lasted less than a year. A few of the girls in my spin class were triathletes, and between their stories of training and racing, it was only a matter of time before I caved. The shenanigans of multi-hour bike rides. The allure of mysterious terms such as "deep dish wheels" and "aero helmets." The camaraderie of training for a common goal come hell or high water or, in many cases, both. It was passive evangelism at its finest. Conversion to triathlon, like the sport itself, is simply a war of attrition.

The Spirit of St. Louis Half Marathon in April of 2006 was the tent meeting that sparked revival. As my spinning posse and I carpooled to the start line, I made a proposition.

"Okay," I joked, "if you get along with me and accept me into your group—if this whole thing works out—I'm gonna buy a road bike today and start doing tris with you."

I said it in jest. I ran the half. The next day, I went out and bought a road bike.

My spinning class instructor went with me to two local bike shops. It was supposed to be a research trip. We would look at some bikes and jot down some information. Instead, several hours and $1,600 later, I emerged from the store, confirmed in the faith by a carbon and aluminum Fuji road warrior. My bike straddled the line between an entry-level acquisition and an all-out purchase, a two-wheeled statement that read, "I could really get into this. I'm not saying I will, but . . . you know. I could."

Initiation into the world of road bikes was slow and, at times, painful. I was grateful for the supportive training wheels of my spin group. Another instructor took me to Creve Coeur Park for my first lesson. In cycling, it's the little things that cause the most trouble. On Kyle's ten-speed, I sat upright on a giant, plush, beanbag of a bike seat. On my new road bike, I was in a lower position, torso bent forward over my elbows. And the seat was smaller. And harder. Stability was another issue. Comfort is sacrificed on the altar of speed, and the low angle of the aero bars—handlebars that require the rider to lean forward over the front of the bike to reduce drag and increase aerodynamic efficiency—is fast but far less stable. In the transition from a recreational bike to one made for racing on the roads, the phrase "It's just like riding a bike" takes on a twisted irony.

The path around the lake at Creve Coeur is four miles long. I barely made one loop. My back was killing me. I felt awkward. I looked even worse. I thought I would never catch on.

But I did. Like so many other challenges in life, getting used to a road bike was a process, and it took time. I'd lug my bike to the paved paths encircling Creve Coeur Lake. I'd make one loop around the lake. Eventually, I could do two. Then three. Slowly and gradually, I improved.

The next year, I returned to the Rec-Plex triathlon for another shot. This time I was prepared. I had started riding with a group of experienced cyclists, and I had joined a triathlon-specific swim class at the YMCA. I amped up my running regimen, chalking off consistent miles on the treadmill at home and at the park behind my house. I even did homework, scouring the internet and bookstores for information on triathlon training, racing, equipment, and nutrition.

I ended up slashing my time in all three legs of the race, with the most significant cut coming on the bike. Real transition areas. Real triathlon clothes. Real road bike. No fashion bathing suit. No locker room break. No towel stuffed in the seat post. I almost felt like a real triathlete.

* * *

Hooker names. That's what we would do. We would use the formula for finding names for professionals of ill-repute—combining the name of your first pet and the name of the street you grew up on—and head to Vegas.

Not long after finishing the Rec-Plex tri, I wrangled several friends into joining me in Las Vegas for the marathon in December. I would run the full. They could run the half. And, to keep the whole thing fun, we would use hooker names all weekend. It would be a hoot!

Over the next several months, we trained for Vegas. We signed up as charity runners to raise money for a mutual friend who had multiple sclerosis. Mimi joined the group as a "manager," adopting the name "Suzette Queens." I, being the

younger sister, deferred to Mimi's firstborn right to Suzette
and was dubbed "TT," or "Trainer Teri." After all, this whole
crazy scheme had been my idea. I would take responsibility in
both name and deed.

Mimi and I were at the airport when I spotted a book
that piqued my interest: *Four Months to a Four-Hour Marathon*.
I bought it and read it on the plane.

We rendezvoused at our hotel and headed to the
marathon expo to pick up our race numbers and runner's
swag. I scanned the booths of vendors for pacing groups. The
book had said that most races provide designated pace groups
headed by an experienced runner. The lead pacer runs with a
sign marked with the designated finish time. All you have to do
is sign up, keep up with the pack, and cross the finish line in your
goal time. I found a four-hour pace group—the time I would
need to qualify for the Boston Marathon—and signed up.

Race morning began at 5:00 a.m. in front of the
palatial golden triad of Mandalay Bay on the south end of the
famous Las Vegas Strip. For six miles, Las Vegas Boulevard
is transformed into a sea of bib numbers, water stops, and
cowbell-ringing spectators. Mimi and Teresa, another friend
who volunteered for managerial duties, collected our post-
race bags and wished us hail and farewell as we found our start
corrals. Then, with the explosion of the starter's pistol, we were
off, and Mimi and Teresa headed straight back to the hotel for
the champagne brunch.

One by one, the girls completed the 13.1 miles,
returning to the finish line to wait for me. They watched the
clock. They knew I had made a last-minute decision to try to
qualify for Boston. Four hours. That's what I needed. The clock
ticked its way upward. I still remember seeing everyone at the

finish line when I crossed. Their arms were raised and they were yelling my name. I was ecstatic. I had done it. 3:57:36.

This whole endurance sport thing, the marathon, triathlon—I was starting to get it. The endorphins. The "runner's high." The fitness. The ability to step out the front door on any given day and run ten, fifteen, even twenty miles. And that was just the tip of the iceberg. The sport went even deeper. I knew it. I had seen it. And I was fascinated.

It was a Saturday afternoon in 2005. The small TV in front of the treadmill was tuned to NBC and the Ironman World Championship in Kona, Hawaii. Tactical editing and a polished narration go a long way in concentrating a seventeen-hour race into a ninety-minute broadcast. The event itself is default reality TV that has no peer. After all, Ironman Kona boasts eighteen hundred[1] of the world's best athletes competing in one of the most grueling endurance races across breathtakingly beautiful and savage terrain. But the salient feature of NBC's coverage of the event—other than the pro athlete reports— are the spotlight vignettes of a handful of extraordinary age groupers, everyday triathletes competing despite insurmountable odds or driven by motivations far greater than the race itself.

I had heard of the Ironman, years before. I knew about the heart-wrenching finishes, of athletes dragging their broken bodies across the finish line. This idea of taking the human body to its physical and mental breaking points resonated with my predisposition to extremes. My drinking had been a personal challenge as much as it had been an addiction. I remember thinking in the midst of my alcoholism, "How much can I drink before my body throws it back up?" If there

---

1   The number of participants in the Ironman World Championship has since increased to over two thousand.

was a limit, I was prone to test it. The concept of the Ironman, then, left an indelible impression in my mind.

Years passed, and the seed lay dormant until that Saturday afternoon when the stories of a vivacious nun and a dying man cracked the soil.

Sister Madonna Buder always had a penchant for unconventionality. Born in 1930, she entered the convent at the age of twenty-three, but eventually left the traditional order for a non-canonical congregation independent of the Catholic Church. Running didn't become part of her routine until she was forty-eight, after a priest suggested she try the sport. Several years later, she completed the first of her forty-six Ironmans (and counting). She was fifty-five.

In 2005, Sister Madonna attempted to become the oldest woman ever to finish an Ironman. The NBC cameras followed her throughout the race, providing a synopsis narration of her life as she rocked a sandy brown Betty White coif and a pair of spandex bike shorts across 140.6 miles. Finally, she crossed the finish line, becoming the oldest female participant to complete an Ironman at the spry young age of seventy-five.

I was drawn to Sister Madonna's story. An older woman flouting both age and expectations to complete an Ironman presented a doable reality. In her own way, Sister Madonna was rebellious. She was extreme. She was a late bloomer. Plus, she was a Visitation Academy graduate.

And then there was Jon Blais.

The NBC narrative deferred to the voice of the man himself, reading a poem as the bright camera lights shined against the final miles of his race. His voice was one of conviction, unfaltering, each word articulated with eerily eulogistic significance. In a business in which time is money and seconds tick away with the corresponding flash of dollar signs, the network had jettisoned standard telecast velocity and stopped the race, metaphorically speaking, to tell the story of the teacher from California. It was a fitting offering for a man who had so little time left of his own.

Originally from the East Coast, Jon Blais moved across the country to earn his masters degree in special education. His passion to inspire and help others led him to the Aseltine School in San Diego, a school for children with emotional disorders and learning disabilities. An athlete who excelled on any playing field, including that of triathlon, Jon incorporated his love for sports into the kids' recreation programs, teaching them the value of perseverance, hard work, and strength of character. In the classroom, Jon focused on improving his students' reading skills, believing that literacy—and the corresponding ability to share in the emotions of others and better communicate their own—would aid in the healing process. "The Blazeman," as the kids called him, was a fixture at Aseltine.

In May of 2005, Jon was diagnosed with amyotrophic lateral sclerosis. ALS, otherwise known as Lou Gehrig's disease, is a death sentence. There is no cure for ALS, and so few advancements have been made in the treatment of the disease that when doctors gave Jon their prognosis, they told him very much the same thing Gehrig's doctors would have said back in 1939. Jon probably had two years to live, maybe five. He was thirty-three.

Shortly after he was diagnosed, Jon moved back home to Massachusetts, where his parents lived. He would need their help. ALS is a particularly cruel disease not only because it blindsides those it strikes with a known and impending expiration date, but also because it strips them of quality of life in the little time they have left. In ALS, nerve cells in the brain and spinal cord die, causing patients to lose control of voluntary muscle movement. Most people with the disease lose control of arm and leg movements first, with initial symptoms manifesting themselves in the hands and feet. The muscle atrophy eventually spreads to the rest of the body, as patients lose the ability to walk, sit up, and hold their heads upright. Speech becomes incomprehensibly slurred and swallowing a dangerous enterprise, if not impossible, as muscles in the face, mouth, and throat degenerate. A feeding tube and a tracheotomy are often needed. Eventually, the muscles in the chest can no longer function, and breathing becomes progressively more difficult until respirators are needed simply for survival. All motor function is lost as the entire central nervous system succumbs to paresis. Because it affects only voluntary muscle function, ALS does not damage the heart. Nor does it affect the brain. ALS patients are completely aware and cognizant as their bodies shut down, even to the very end. It is a callous and merciless disease, one that shortens life and prolongs death. Those with ALS are front-row witnesses to their own slow, systematic paralysis. Simply put, with ALS, you watch yourself die.

Jon Blais was not going to be a bystander. Ever the athlete, he had long dreamed of competing in an Ironman. Now, with the window of possibility quickly closing, he applied for a spot in the Ironman World Championship. He knew his time of physical autonomy was limited. The race was in five months. It would be cutting it close.

By the time race day arrived, the disease had already severely compromised Jon's body. His entire left side was slowly succumbing to paralysis. His left quad and gluteus muscles were completely numb. He could no longer control his hands with any dexterity, making even tying his shoelaces an impossible task. His left arm was useless, and he had to Velcro it to his bike to keep it from sliding off the handlebar. His bike also had to be modified with special grips and braces so that he could operate it using only his right side. Though he once was an elite competitor, his only goal now was to finish within the allotted seventeen hours—even if, as he famously phrased it, he had to roll himself across the finish.

Which is exactly what he did. Conquering the 140.6 miles with over thirty minutes to spare, Jon dropped to the ground and rolled the final inches across the coveted finish line. It was a deliberate act of victory and defiance. It was a call to arms. Jon Blais became the first and only person with ALS to complete an Ironman, and in doing so, he gave a face to a disease that for too long had relied on the shadows for its existence.

I cried as I watched the race. I was sitting on the floor of the basement, my workout finished. I knew. Someday— someday—I would be an Ironman. Someday, I would do this great thing.

The following year, Jon returned to Kona. The trip was extremely difficult. The disease had progressed rapidly, and his body, which only twelve months before had been strong, young, and able, was now withered and confined to a wheelchair.

But Jon had declared war, and a warrior's life belongs to the battlefield. In 2005, he had led the charge. In 2006, he challenged others to take up the standard.

And in 2007, he was gone.

5

GOING 140.6

M ost people just don't get it. The time. The effort. The money. The inconvenience. The pain. The asceticism. The commitment. The sacrifice. They just don't get it.

And these are the people who know what an Ironman is.

Not many people can look at a race that takes place over 140.6 miles in a single day and say, "Yeah, I wanna do that." A 2.4-mile swim followed by a 112-mile bike followed by a 26.2-mile run. Back-to-back-to-back. It's as though the events and the miles are packed on gratuitously—spitefully, almost. A seventeen-hour time limit is added, just for good measure. Finish in under seventeen hours—and not one second over—or your race won't count. Those who do an Ironman will surely suffer, for suffering is par for the Ironman course. They will hurt, they will bleed, they will sweat, they will cry, they will ache, and they will cramp; they will pull something, tweak something, lose something, strain something, or break something (body part or equipment); they will most likely puke, pee on themselves, chafe in embarrassing places, or be afflicted with all sorts of other inglorious maladies, many of them related to the gastrointestinal system; they will, at one point or another, be nauseated, fatigued, dizzy, dehydrated, and utterly depleted.

People who want to do an Ironman know this. They've seen it. They've read about it. They've had friends and coworkers and family members and training partners tell them about it. They know the horror stories. That's not the problem. They know what it takes to get to the finish line.

What they don't know is what it takes to reach the start.

Jeff Eddy hears it all the time. As an athletic trainer, triathlon coach, and strength and conditioning specialist, he is inundated with Ironman hopefuls, wannabes, and dreamers. They come to him with their hopes and aspirations, the starry-eyed masses yearning for the title of Ironman. They envision themselves worthy of the "M-Dot," the sacred symbol of the Ironman, so called because of its rather clever design that uses a strategically placed dot to transform the capital M of the Ironman logo into a believable torso of a man. Brilliant because of its simplicity, hallowed because of what it signifies, the M-Dot is not just another trademark. The Ironman M-Dot does not say, "I was there," or "I know someone who was there." The M-Dot says, "I crossed the finish line." It is not a statement to be taken lightly.

Once you earn the M-Dot, it is yours forever. You pull it over your head, you slap it on your car, you wear it around your neck, you tattoo it on your skin. It tells a story. It says, "I have been to hell and back in 140.6 miles." But until you actually grace the fiery gates of endurance sport and live to tell about it, the M-Dot is strictly off-limits. You don't buy it. You don't wear it. You don't touch it.

But you think about it. And you dream. And you covet. To swim and bike and run your way to one of the most epic finish lines in sport. To hear your name followed by the triumphant declaration, "You are . . . an Ironman!" To have the medal placed around your neck. Yes, you most certainly think about it. You picture yourself there. And, caught up in the euphoric imaginations of what it would be like to have access to such a sacrosanct trademark, you call Jeff Eddy.

And in three seconds, he cuts you back down to size.

I had heard about Jeff and his wife through the triathlon grapevine. The Eddys were members at the gym. When I approached Jeff's wife, Trish, about training for an Ironman, Trish directed me back to Jeff. He was the expert. After a brief introduction, I made the declaration he had heard so many times before.

"I want to do an Ironman."

Jeff launched into his standard verbal questionnaire. What kind of training had I done in the past? What races had I done? What were my short-term goals? What were my long-term goals?

I recapped my brief career. At that point, I had run two marathons and completed some Olympic distance triathlons. I thought I had earned my brownie points.

"I was thinking I could do Ironman Louisville next September," I said.

"Sorry . . . you have to do a half Ironman first."

Jeff. Ever the reality check.

It was fall of 2006. Jeff suggested I make Ironman Louisville 2008 my goal. If I wanted to make the jump to the Ironman, I had some work to do.

After running Boston in April, I signed up for the Redman Triathlon half Ironman distance in Oklahoma City. Once again, I recruited Jeff to coach me.

Jeff's confidence in my ability to master at least two of the three disciplines was high. My strong swim background gave me an obvious advantage, as did my Boston Marathon qualification. The bike, on the other hand, was another story.

The first time Jeff saw me on a bike, he asked where the third wheel was. I wasn't steady at all. He said I was like a newborn giraffe—twitchy and uncertain. Even now I prefer to sit upright and "ride the bullhorns" instead of leaning forward on the aero bars. Riding the bullhorns is fine for leisurely clips around the block, but when your training rides jump to sixty, eighty, and one hundred miles, you need to be as aerodynamic and energy-efficient as possible. The science is simple: the lower you are, the less wind you'll fight. Jeff concocted a training recipe designed to improve my bike skills.

On September 23, 2007, I completed the Redman half Ironman distance in Oklahoma. I felt good about the race and immediately set my sights on Ironman Louisville 2008. Maintaining a strong aerobic base throughout the fall, I got a running start—quite literally—into the tri season, returning to Boston in April for a second dance with the Boston Marathon before diving headfirst into full Ironman training.

And if there is one idea that Ironman trainees must not only accept but embrace with unadulterated devotion, it is the linchpin concept of committing to the jump.

Dave and I decided from the start that my training wouldn't take over our lives. I would train while Kati was at school and Dave was at work (by this time, Kyle was away at college). It was one way I could buck the trend of imposition.

The heaviest toll that all Ironman hopefuls must pay is time. And it's a doozie. Detailed and methodical time management becomes a necessary skill as you manipulate your schedule to fit at least three swim workouts, three or four bike rides, and five or more runs into your weekly routine. The math is simple. Eleven or twelve workouts in seven days means two-a-days are a necessary evil, whether the workouts are split between morning and evening or stacked on top of each other in a "brick." Long gone are the weeks with single-digit hours of training, the thirty-minute runs, the twenty-mile long rides, the quick dips in the pool. Those are promptly chewed apart and consumed by fifteen hours of training during low mileage weeks and up to twenty-five hours of training during peak weeks. And that's just aerobic time. Once training commences, you live and breath Ironman. If you're not actually in the middle of a workout, you're driving to or from one, preparing for one, fueling for one, or thinking about one.

Like many training schedules, my itinerary included several key triathlons leading up to Louisville. In May, I would race an Olympic distance tri in Memphis. In June, I would head to Kansas for a half Ironman. July would see another half Ironman in Muncie, Indiana.

I started my week on the bike. Forty-five miles and lots of hills. Over the spring I had started riding with Big Shark

Bicycle Company, a local bike store that organized group rides. Through Big Shark, I met some of my dearest training friends: Cristel Santiago, a feisty Puerto Rican with strong coffee hair and an even stronger personality; her husband, Ruben Aymerich, also from Puerto Rico and a gastroenterologist at St. John's Hospital; and PJ and Joe Walsh, a power couple of cycling. They would all become frontline soldiers in my army after my diagnosis.

On Tuesdays, I would swim and run. The pool was home to me. Rarely did I swim less than two or three miles.

On Wednesdays, it was back on the bike, usually for sixty or seventy miles, give or take a dozen. I'd haul my bike out west and meet up with Cristel and PJ to ride the hills of Wildwood. Later in the evening, I'd trudge down to the basement for forty-five minutes of weight training.

Thursdays were brick workouts: an eight-mile run and a two-hour bike. I ran my long runs on Fridays, usually during the hottest part of the day. I'd even throw on extra clothes, pulling on two shirts or a jacket, just to raise the temperature. I like the heat. I think I thrive on it, which is a good thing. Heat training prepared me for the sweltering August temperatures of Louisville and, later, Kona.

I saved my lightest workouts for Saturdays, which were devoted to family time. And on Sundays I'd rendezvous with Jeff and another of his athletes-in-training, Scott Stern. Scott was a mutual friend who was also training for an Ironman, and each weekend the three of us would meet up in Lake St. Louis for seventy or eighty miles on the bike and a post-ride run.

I like to keep my training simple. For me, training boils down to mileage. On any given workout, I'll lock into a rhythm and crank out the miles, even if it means neglecting a pace-specific assignment. Once I get going, I'm a one-pace kind of girl. I prefer to just listen to my body. If I feel good, I'll run hard. If I am struggling, I'll slow down. Just as long as I get in the miles, I am happy. I didn't know it then, but this streamlined approach, one based on the enjoyment of just being active, would be key to success when I was training through cancer treatment.

Jeff, Scott, and I coordinated workouts and tune-up races when we could. The miles have a way of accelerating friendships, as does mutual misery, and it didn't take long for the three of us to realize something unique was forming as we carried each other through tough workouts, shared each other's highs and lows, and laughed at inside jokes. Still, Jeff, Scott, and I didn't become the trio that we are until the road trip to Muncie.

I had known Scott since 1985, when he first met Dave through the mortgage banking industry. After Scott joined me under the tutelage of Jeff Eddy, we gained the camaraderie of a shared passion. Still, our friendship was tagged with the middleman label of client and friend-by-association. We were cordial, but still a bit stiff. If we were going to be spending all of this time together—including a ten-hour roundtrip car ride and a weekend in Indiana—this formality, this decorum, these professional niceties, Scott decided, needed to end.

Scott's method of breaking the ice was risky—he wasn't sure how I would react—but at least I would know the real him. After all, what is propriety if not the fear of offending someone?

"Look," he said once the three of us were piled into his car, "I feel like I need to say something. Teri, there's something I need to say to you . . ."

He then unleashed an unprecedented fusillade of expletives—every cuss word or combination of cuss words he could think of—which is saying something, considering Scott has one of the more impressive verbal arsenals around. It was the most random outburst of profanity, and it took me completely off guard. I couldn't stop laughing. I think if it had been someone else, I would have been offended. But this was so Scott.

In that moment, Scott and I became dear friends. He began calling me his "triathlon wife." I began calling Jeff and Scott my "triathlon husbands." We had formed some kind of weird club.

I had a strong race in Muncie. My time of five hours, twenty minutes, placed me third in my age group and would have qualified me for the 70.3 Ironman World Championship in Clearwater, Florida, had Muncie been an official Ironman event. Riding the coattails of my surprising performance, I headed to Louisville.

Luckily, the coattails were big. Over fifteen people traveled to the race to cheer me on, including Dave, Kyle, Kati, Mimi, Laverne, my nieces, and the Eddys. Louisville was a family affair, and not devoid of chaos.

The race started at 7:00 a.m. I had planned on making my way down to the race early. I wanted plenty of time to set up my transition areas and check my bike one final time before heading to the swim start a half-mile away. But leaving the hotel wasn't quite as smooth of a process as I could have hoped, and I ended up being the very last participant to arrive at the bike transition area—T1 as it is called. In fact, I was the only person in the bike transition area. Everyone else had already checked their gear and headed downstream, so to speak, to the start. Panicked, I rushed through the final preparation rituals, but I didn't even get to check my tires before race officials announced that T1 was closed. Once the announcement is made, all participants must leave the area or face disqualification. I abandoned my bike and found Jeff. I will never forget standing in the transition area before the race, the last athlete out. I was so frazzled.

When I finally made the walk from the transition area to the swim start on the docks along the Ohio River, I faced a single-file line 2,200 athletes long. Not only is Louisville a point-to-point swim, which means athletes enter and exit the water at different locations, but it has a rolling start: athletes line up on a first come, first served basis and jump into the water one by one, in one- or two-second intervals. Like so many things in the world of Ironman, the swim start in Louisville is a numbers game. It takes approximately forty-five minutes to get all the participants in the water.

In addition to being the only participant in the transition area, I was also the only participant (at least as far as I could tell) who wore a regular Speedo swimsuit for the swim instead of a swimskin suit, which you wear over your racing clothes to reduce drag. Instead, I jumped into the Ohio River in a rainbow-colored, flower-printed one-piece and wasted quite a bit of time in the transition area changing into the clothes I would wear for the rest of the race.

But despite its inauspicious beginnings, Ironman Louisville was a success. First and foremost, I finished. Second, I did so in twelve hours, seventeen minutes. Cheered on by family, friends, and hundreds of strangers, I was baptized into triathlon's most elite club.

"Teri Griege! You . . . are . . . an . . . Ironman!"

Completing an Ironman was something I had wanted to do for a long time. I was so grateful to be out there every single minute of every single mile. When I crossed that finish line, all I could think was, "How cool is this? How cool is it to be able to do this?" The race left me with a sense of accomplishment: I had set a goal, and I had achieved it.

Louisville left an indelible mark, as Ironmans always do. I never got the 140.6 sticker for my car or an M-Dot tattoo, but I loved to talk about it. (If you asked me about it, I'd never shut up.) Louisville also stirred up a new level of competition, one I hadn't anticipated or even considered a possibility. In my debut Ironman, I had missed qualifying for the World Championship by just one slot.

My training had been founded on three principles: have fun, don't get bored, and don't take anything too seriously. But Louisville presented me with a new reality of training for an ambitious goal. The sudden prospect of racing with the best in the world was startling.

After Louisville, I shifted my focus to the Ironman World Championship in Kona. I would train harder, train better, and return to Louisville to earn my spot on the Big Island.

Goals change quickly. Motivations evolve. What once seemed extreme suddenly becomes pedestrian. The only way to stay challenged is to find another, steeper gradient. For me, that next level was Kona.

After returning to Vegas to run the marathon at the end of 2008, I ran the GO! St. Louis Marathon several months later in April. I also decided to repeat the same quartet of triathlons I had raced the year before: Memphis in May (Olympic distance), Ironman Kansas 70.3 in June, Muncie Endurathon (half Ironman distance) in early July, and

Ironman Louisville in late August. Jeff, Scott, and I continued our Sunday morning services at Lake St. Louis, coordinating our training and racing schedules.

Even so, my training for my second Ironman was iffy, at best. First, there was the foot injury that refused to heal. I had been nursing it for months, but by early summer the pain had become severe enough that I needed prescription anti-inflammatories. I received two cortisone shots—one before Ironman Kansas 70.3 in late June and the other before Louisville. But despite my efforts, at the half Ironman in Kansas, the injury forced me to do something I had never before done in a race: drop out. I was only a mile and a half into the run, but the foot pain was severe. I felt as though I were running on a sharp rock. I pulled up and walked off the course. I didn't want to risk further injury by continuing the race and then be unable to compete in Louisville, which was less than two months away.

Then there was the fatigue. It wasn't constant, but it was frequent. The pop in my legs wasn't there. I couldn't keep up with Jeff and Scott on the bike. It was strange and a bit discouraging, but still only occasional. Some days I felt tired, but others I would feel great and hammer a workout. I figured I had over-trained and was simply another year older.

Two months after Kansas, I returned to Ironman Louisville. Though I had signed up for the event with the goal of qualifying for Kona, the reality of a suboptimal training season pared down my expectations heading into the race. Even as I jumped into the water, I knew I wasn't going to qualify unless my body managed to pull a massive performance out of nowhere.

I had a strong swim—I managed to cover the distance one minute faster than I had the year before. But once I got on the bike, where the lingering fatigue had been most noticeable, I knew the day was going to be a long one. One by one, people passed me as I dropped further back in the race. Near the end of the 112-mile bike course, two women whom I recognized whooshed by. It was a disheartening pass. They weren't strong swimmers, or particularly strong cyclists for that matter.

I saw JoAnn as I crossed a bridge just outside the second transition area. I had taken longer on the bike than expected. I knew she would be worried.

"Oh, honey, how are you feeling? Are you gonna be okay on the run?" she yelled as I ran by. She could tell I was struggling.

I didn't feel great, but I never felt like I couldn't keep running. I was just slower. And twelve hours, twenty-seven minutes after I jumped into the waters of the Ohio River, I was just glad to be done. Kona, at least for now, would have to wait.

Still, I was satisfied with my performance. I had known the race was going to be rough. I knew I was fatigued. I knew my body wasn't healing, wasn't recovering, wasn't quite right. I thought I had over-trained. I thought I was just getting older.

I didn't think I was dying.

6

THE CANCER WITHIN

M imi made me go to the doctor.

She was at our house. We were going to lunch, and I used the bathroom before we headed out. Mimi followed suit. As soon as she walked into the bathroom, she noticed it. There was blood in the toilet. A lot of it. She marched right back out.

"Teri, I don't know what's wrong with you, but you have got to go see someone," she said, the concern evident on her face.

"Yeah, I know. I will."

I wasn't worried. At least, not really. Louisville was only a week removed. I had just taxed my body to the highest degree. I had heard of endurance athletes experiencing blood in their stools due to hemorrhoids or intestinal ischemia—a condition in which the body diverts blood from the digestive tract to the muscles, causing the intestinal lining to slough and the blood vessels beneath to bleed—and hadn't I just completed an Ironman? In fact, wasn't I always asking my body to give more after intense workouts in the pool, on the bike, on the roads, or all of the above? Some blood in my stool may not have been normal, but certainly it wasn't unheard of.

Then again, this wasn't the first time. That had been two months earlier, at the beginning of July. I had gone to the bathroom only to see a dark red cloud mushroom across the water in the toilet bowl. I was startled, but not necessarily concerned. I figured there was a logical, harmless explanation. The anti-inflammatories, for example. I had been taking them all summer because of my foot injury. With a heavy training and racing workload, I didn't have the time or patience for such things as injuries, especially those that didn't so much incapacitate as inconvenience. By the time I noticed any rectal bleeding in July, I attributed it to the medicine, which had already been tearing up my stomach. Plus, the bleeding was sporadic. Some days I had it; some days I didn't. Occasionally, it was very painful.

Neither of the issues—the fatigue or the bleeding—was constant or unbearable. For every bad workout, I had two good ones. It was like a car that sputters intermittently but performs with hot rod precision when brought to the mechanic. Sure, I had struggled through Ironman Kansas 70.3 in June, but a month later I had raced the half iron distance in Muncie and felt just fine. Each incident was isolated, insubstantial, and forgettable. Anything that could have been cause for concern simply wasn't.

Looking back, I see these symptoms for what they were, but it took a long time for me to notice. I remember long runs at Creve Coeur Lake in which I'd run fifteen or sixteen miles, and I felt like I had buckets of cement on my feet. But it wasn't every time. Some days I'd have a really great run. On other days it took everything I had just to finish. But, like you do with everything else, you adapt over time. Especially with endurance athletes. You train to endure pain. You train to endure fatigue. When you feel bad, you don't let it get to you. You just deal with it. And so I did. Through training. Through Louisville. After Louisville. Even when the persistence of the rectal bleeding caused a vague uneasiness—I had stopped taking the anti-inflammatories several weeks before—I never thought to go to the doctor. But Mimi was adamant. This wasn't normal. I had to see somebody. Finally, I acquiesced.

I decided I would bring up the issue to Cristel's husband Ruben, who was a gastroenterologist. He had ridden with our cycling group before, but only a handful of times. By chance, just days after Mimi's visit, he joined Cristel, PJ, Joe, and me for a ride on the Katy Trail. His presence seemed fortuitous. I would ask him during the ride.

Mile after mile passed. Still, I didn't say anything. We talked about training, equipment, and races. I told myself I'd bring up the topic when there was a break in the conversation. I'd ask him in five minutes. In ten minutes. In another ten. But I couldn't get the nerve. I just didn't feel comfortable talking about such a personal, embarrassing subject. The ride ended. I never said anything.

Afterwards, I headed to the pool. Even as I swam, I felt unsettled. What was the matter with me? This was ridiculous. Why was I so scared?

I called Ruben as soon as I got home. He suggested we do a colonoscopy and told me to call his office. As it turned out, Ruben was booked several weeks out, but Cristel, propelled by an unexplainable sense of urgency, was able to get me in for an appointment forty-eight hours later.

Because sedation is standard procedure for colonoscopies, I needed a chauffeured ride home from my appointment. Dave would be at the airport picking up his brother Chuck, who was flying in from Dallas for a golf tournament. I called Mimi.

Still, I didn't say anything to anyone else. I didn't even tell Dave I was going in for a colonoscopy until the night before. I knew the blood wasn't right. I had been a nurse, after all, and I knew the symptoms of potential trouble. But the whole thing was embarrassing. I wasn't one to go around talking about blood in my poop.

The day before the procedure, I began the litany of preparation. After a small breakfast, I started my fast: nothing but clear liquids until after the test. Later that evening, I would have to take a series of laxatives—"dynamite pills," as I called them—to clear my bowels.

Kati and I giggled the whole night when I was going through the prep. It all seemed funny. The day before the colonoscopy I was a bit nervous—there was enough uncertainty in my head—but I didn't think anything of it. I didn't know what to make of it.

September 17. Thursday.

Mimi picked me up at 8:00 a.m. Dave was at the office, sneaking in an hour of work before collecting Chuck at the airport and heading to Greenbriar. Kyle was away at college. Kati was in school.

We live only three miles from the hospital, and soon Mimi and I were walking across the sprawling parking lot toward the main entrance of St. John's. We made our way into the large lobby with its labyrinth of corridors, each one categorized by ailment or body part. But our search was quick. The GI lab was a left turn away.

The room was crowded and quiet and mechanically coordinated from floor to ceiling with processed floral patterns. The coat hanger just to the right of the door was empty; I remember it was warm that day.

I walked up to the receptionist's desk, checked in, and began filling out paperwork. The nurse gave me a blue pager. The first beep would let me know it was my turn; all subsequent beeps would alert Mimi of my progress.

We didn't wait long before the buzzer went off. I passed the device to Mimi and followed the nurse through the door to the nucleus of the GI lab. Nearly thirty individual bays, separated by curtains, lined the walls, each one numbered and stocked with a single stretcher. The nurse led me to bay number six, where I undressed and donned the striped, light blue hospital gown that had been folded up on the stretcher. I tossed my black Nike pants and tech running shirt in a bag and lay down. A run sounded good right then. Or a ride. Either one, really. The weather was too gorgeous to be trapped in the antiseptic confines of the GI lab. At any rate, the sooner I got home, the better. Later that evening, Dave and I, along with Dave and Kathy Diemer, were hosting a bridge dedication at Greenbriar in honor of the men's fathers.

Both families had been members of Greenbriar since the 1960s and highly involved in the club's operations. Charles Griege had been president in 1981, one year before being diagnosed with leukemia. He died the next year. In 2001, Peter Diemer, a radiologist, was diagnosed with the same type of leukemia from which Dr. Griege had suffered. In 2007, he succumbed to the disease and passed away. For years we had discussed doing something at the club to honor Dr. Griege and Dr. Diemer. When the golf course underwent a few cosmetic procedures in 2008, we saw our opportunity in the dedication of a new bridge. The evening was going to be special, and it had been long in the making.

But for now, I was temporarily incarcerated in bay number six. The nurse returned to complete the final preparation. Ruben stopped by to see if I had any questions.

"Don't worry," he said smiling. "It will be easy, and you'll get a good nap. It's probably some hemorrhoids or something."

I shook my head. "I don't think this is hemorrhoids."

The succession of medical staff continued as Ruben left and the anesthesiologist appeared. Another pop quiz on my medical history, another review of the procedure. Finally, I was collected from the bay and wheeled down the hall. The anesthesiologist began asking me questions about running. I rolled onto my left side and brought my knees to my chest, the position in which I'd remain during the colonoscopy. The anesthetic was pumped in. I talked about my last marathon. It was a short conversation. Within fifteen seconds, I was asleep. U2 was playing on the radio. Mimi sat in the waiting room, reading a magazine. Kyle was in Texas. Kati was in school. Dave was at the airport.

He saw it right away. The growth wasn't subtle. There was no uncertainty, no need to wait for diagnostic results. He hadn't expected this. It was cancer, and it was advanced.

Ruben had just started the colonoscopy when he found the large, donut-shaped tumor centimeters above my rectum. A colonoscopy is unglamorous business, to say the least. A six-foot-long colonoscope, similar in appearance to a thin, black garden hose and outfitted with a light and a small camera, is navigated backwards through the entire length of the colon to the cecum, where the large and small intestines meet. The scope's inward journey is relatively quick—about five or six minutes. The second half of the procedure takes longer, with the actual examination of the colon taking place as the scope is pulled back out. For a healthy colon without any growths, the whole procedure lasts twenty to thirty minutes; if a polyp is found and a biopsy is needed, more time is required.

In my case, the tumor was so low in the rectum that Ruben saw it immediately. It was also large—the size of a small orange, perforated in the middle. The colonoscope didn't fit through the small opening in the tumor, which was a problem since Ruben needed to search for more growths further down my colon. Switching to a pediatric colonoscope, he was able to navigate the smaller tube through the opening. Growths usually begin on one side of the intestinal wall and expand around the circumference of the colon. Left untreated, a tumor will continue to grow in both directions until the ends of the growth connect, forming a ring, or "donut," as mine had. The size of the tumor in relation to the late onset and subtlety of my symptoms meant that it had grown quickly, probably within the year. Because the cancer was so aggressive, Ruben worried that it had already metastasized to other nearby organs, specifically, the liver, where the blood supply that drains the lower bowels travels first, leaving the organ susceptible in the anatomic progression of the disease.

Colon cancer is tricky because it is silent. It doesn't trigger noticeable symptoms until the disease is critically advanced. Even then, there may be no symptoms at all. Those that do appear are both so subtle and varied that most people notice them only upon looking back after diagnosis. A little fatigue here and there. Anemia, maybe. By the time rectal bleeding occurs—if it does at all—the diagnosis is usually dire. I was within months of dying without ever knowing I was sick. My fatigue was explained away. So was the bleeding. And I wasn't anemic at all.

This last fact is noteworthy. Your bone marrow is responsible for producing red blood cells. Your body regulates red blood cell count by sending chemical signals to the bone marrow, telling it the necessary rate of production. When you lose large amounts of blood, your body has to work harder to maintain the correct level. My body was responding so efficiently to the demand for more blood that it masked the symptoms of my cancer, even during intense Ironman training.

Ruben finished the colonoscopy, snagging a specimen from the tumor for a biopsy and sending it off to the lab for further testing. Immediately, he called the radiology department and ordered a CT scan of my abdomen to check for tumors in my liver, spleen, and stomach. He hung up the phone. He hadn't expected this. He hadn't expected it to be anything remarkable.

But it was.

Mimi was there when I woke up in the recovery room. The beeper had gone off as soon as the procedure was finished.

We chatted for a few minutes. Just small talk. The anesthesiologist stopped by and told us Ruben had done a biopsy. He didn't say anything else.

Within a few minutes, Ruben walked into our bay and stood next to the bed.

"Teri, I have some bad news. It's unexpected." He took a breath. "I have to be straight with you. We didn't get very far, and we found a tumor."

Mimi and I listened as Ruben elaborated on the diagnosis. It was definitely cancer, but they were going to send it to the pathology department for more testing. The good news was that the tumor was operable. Also, he wanted a few more blood tests as well as a CT scan, which he'd already scheduled for later that day.

I immediately pictured myself with a colostomy bag. It was my only thought. The cancer diagnosis went completely over my head.

"Will I need a colostomy?"

Ruben didn't think so.

"Listen," he said after he had explained the basic facets of the diagnosis, "if you want me to call Dave for you, I'll call Dave."

"No, don't call Dave. He's in a golf tournament, and it will ruin his day."

Ruben was flabbergasted. "Teri, that's your husband. If I was your husband and you didn't tell me, I'd be pissed."

I looked at Ruben. I don't think his words had registered in my brain yet. I could sense it was painful for him to deliver the bad news, but I felt separate from it, as if it had nothing to do with me.

"This must be so hard for you," I said.

"Teri," he said, trying to break through my wall of self-denial, "it's your turn to be the patient."

Mimi asked a few more questions. Then she called Dave.

Dave and Chuck were in a golf cart heading back from the driving range to have lunch at the club when Dave's cell phone buzzed.

"Dave, it's Mimi. We've got a problem. They found a tumor in Teri's colon. She has cancer."

Dave fabricated an excuse about a problem at the office and headed to St. John's. When he got there, Ruben repeated my diagnosis, giving a few more details about the tests he wanted to run. They carted me off to the radiology department for a CT scan. They wouldn't know the results until later that evening. I still thought this was all just precautionary protocol. There was no point in Dave staying around the hospital, especially since Mimi was there. Chuck was in town. People at the club would be wondering what in the world was going on. I told Dave to head back to Greenbriar. I would meet him there.

It was late by the time Mimi brought me home. The house was quiet and dark. I tossed my purse on the counter and sat down at the computer. I looked at the clock. The ceremony at Greenbriar started in thirty minutes. I didn't have much time.

Colon cancer. Colon cancer stages. Colon cancer survival rate. Colon cancer treatment. I rummaged through different websites, stopped to read, and then searched some more. What I found wasn't encouraging. I didn't know exactly how bad my diagnosis was—the details would come with the test results later that evening—but I knew it was advanced. Ruben had said that much.

Any positive statistics were isolated to the early stages of the cancer. Patients diagnosed with Stage I colon cancer have a five-year survival rate of 74 percent. From there, it is a sharp drop-off. I scrolled down the page. Stage II. Stage III. Finally, Stage IV, the most advanced stage of the disease. Average survival of patients after diagnosis: two years. The odds that they will make it past five years: 6 percent.[1] I stared at the screen. Only then did my diagnosis sink in. For the first time, I realized the battle I was facing.

I pushed my chair back from the computer and stood up. I felt sick. I felt numb. It was time to head to Greenbriar. I still needed to change.

Back at the hospital, Ruben had just received the results of my CT scan. As he had feared, the cancer had metastasized. He opened up my file on the computer to see the x-ray for himself. The radiologists had provided a very descriptive report. There were not one but two large masses on my liver, most likely tumors. They would have to run the biopsy to confirm the exact diagnosis and staging of the cancer. Even then, its full extent would be known only once surgery was performed. But at that point, further tests were mere technicalities. Colon cancer metastasizes to other organs only when it is in its final and most advanced stage. Ruben looked at the computer screen again. The image left no room for equivocation. I had Stage IV colon cancer.

---

1   From the 7th edition of the AJCC staging manual (2010) and cited on the American Cancer Society website. Statistics reflect observed survival rates of people who were treated at least five years before the study and include colon cancer patients who may have died from other causes. Because many colon cancer patients are older and have preexisting serious health conditions, and because of advancements in colon cancer treatments, actual survival rates are likely to be higher than the numbers indicate.

I stood smiling on the red brick terrace at Greenbriar, surrounded by family and friends. Only a few hours had passed since we had found out I had cancer. We still didn't know the rest of the test results. And now Dave was spearheading a dedication ceremony to honor his own father who had died of cancer. Charles Griege and Peter Diemer were both stalwart patriarchs, both respected doctors, both leaders in the community. The bridge was a testament to the remarkable lives they had lived—and lost to leukemia.

Dave spoke. I stood there. Nobody around us knew. The whole situation was morbid and ironic. I was utterly numb.

But Dave Diemer sensed something was wrong. He had seen me talking with his wife, Kathy, on the patio at the clubhouse. He could tell something was up. He pulled Dave aside, and while the rest of the group made champagne toasts and feasted on hors d'oeuvres, Dave quietly relayed the small bits of information he had about my diagnosis. Diemer was stunned, but there was little time for questions or comfort. The party was ending, and the two returned to their duties as hosts, shaking hands and thanking everyone for coming.

We had planned a post-dedication dinner at the clubhouse with a group of immediate family members: Kati, Dave's mom, his brother Chuck, his brother Jeff; Jeff's wife, Jenny, and their twin daughters, Emily and Sarah; and Dave's sister Kathy. Of the group, only Chuck knew. By this time, even trying to carry on a normal conversation was too much. The strain of keeping up a cheerful front compounded the anxiety of not knowing my full diagnosis. I was still waiting for Ruben's call. I just wanted to go home.

Shortly after the entrees arrived, my phone rang. I stood up and excused myself from the table.

"Teri," Ruben's voice cut through the speakers, "unfortunately this is more advanced than we thought."

I found an empty lounge area adjacent to the main dining room and sat down.

"Teri," he continued. "We found two tumors on your liver."

"So, what does that mean?"

"It means it's a more complicated picture. It's more spread out."

The room was empty, quiet except for the muffled chatter from the other room where my family sat eating and laughing, unsuspecting of the devastating news. Their voices filtered through the heavy wooden doors. I pressed the phone against my ear. I didn't see the tumors. I didn't see the cancer. I didn't see the hospital or the chemo or the painful days ahead. Not yet.

In that moment, I saw only Kati.

She was wearing a long white dress and standing in front of a mirror, smiling—glowing. It was her wedding day. Mimi and JoAnn were standing next to her, their own smiles reflected in the mirror as they admired the young bride before them. They told her how beautiful she looked and how proud I would be if I could only see her, if I were only alive. The vision was clear and vivid. My daughter was getting married, and I was dead.

I began crying.

"Listen," Ruben said, his voice solemn but reassuring, "I don't want you to think that this is a death sentence. I want you to think of this as moving from a half Ironman to a full Ironman."

By this time, Dave had gotten up from the table to look for me. I had been gone over twenty minutes. Dave searched the clubhouse, traversing the long hallways linking parlors and dining rooms. The moment he saw my face, he knew.

He waited while I finished the conversation. I hung up the phone and relayed what Ruben had told me. Ruben would call later with more details. Dave pulled me into a silent embrace, and we cried.

But we couldn't say anything to our family—not yet, not until we knew more. Plus, Kati was there. This was no place for her to find out. We had to put up a front just a little bit longer. We had to pretend like nothing was wrong. We had to compose ourselves. We dried our tears, plastered on smiles, and returned to the table.

Still, the weight and suddenness of the diagnosis was too much. All I knew was that I had to get out of there, that I had to go home. After a few minutes, I offered a brief explanation that I wasn't feeling well and left. Dave would follow after dinner ended.

We weren't home long before Ruben called again. I switched the call to speakerphone. Ruben's accent filtered through the receiver and echoed across the basement where we sat. The test results were indisputable. The cancer had metastasized. I had two large tumors in my liver. It was very serious.

"But it's doable," he said, encouraging us even as he acknowledged the grim reality. "We can do this."

The whole conversation lasted less than ten minutes. Dave hung up the phone. The race in Louisville seemed a million miles away. Things had changed.

Mortality has a way of shattering our reality and resetting the scales. It is a sudden and startling realignment. Our own dimensions, which previously spilled over the horizon with panoramic consumption, are unceremoniously cut down to scale. We become aware of our own smallness. We become aware of our own transience. We become very, very human.

7

THE FIRST DAYS

ew things in life are quick, clean-cut, or simple. Neither were the days following my diagnosis. I was still a wife, a mother, a daughter, a sister, a niece, a friend, and a training partner, and the ramifications of my diagnosis extended deep into the lives of others. I had called Mimi and JoAnn after hanging up the phone with Ruben. The next day, JoAnn called her daughter Julie, who was a nurse in interventional radiology at Barnes Jewish Hospital in St. Louis. Julie knew all the oncologists and surgeons at Barnes. She handpicked an all-star team of doctors and began arranging a stacked itinerary of appointments and meetings for the next day, a turnaround that would have otherwise been impossible.

The circle of those privy to the diagnosis remained small, but it was growing. Still, Kyle and Kati didn't know. Dave and I wanted more information before we told the kids.

The liver surgeon, Dr. William Chapman, materialized the shred of hope first offered by Ruben: the diagnosis was not necessarily a death sentence. He did so by sketching out a methodical plan to attack the cancer. The good news was that the two egg-sized tumors in my liver were operable. The bad news was that they were opposite each other. Dr. Chapman would have to operate on both sides of my liver; the surgery would not be simple. But he and another specialist would brainstorm the best way to remove the tumors while preserving as much of the liver as possible. There was hope.

Dave and I left Barnes and headed west to my mom's. Mimi and JoAnn were already there. They had arrived early to break the news. Now it was my turn.

Born to John and Ida Klingenhagen in 1924, my mom entered a familial milieu of strong German bodies and even stronger personalities. Her mother, Ida Petri, was one of six kids and lived a vibrant and robust one hundred and two years. Ida's approach to life was simultaneously thorough and cavalier. She lived by the motto that if you can't change something, you must simply make the best of it and run. When she passed away in 1999, she was just six months shy of having lived in three centuries.

My mom's father was one of seven children. He fought in World War I, where he spent his time in Germany fighting the Central Powers and playing a good amount of baseball. When he lost his job at a local brewery during Prohibition, he supported his family as a shortstop on a minor league baseball team. He also snagged a day job at the post office and a night gig as a mechanic.

John and Ida instilled in their children the German resilience and stoic industry with which they had been raised. Laverne's older brother Jack was all of five feet, six inches (on a good day), and, at one point, was the youngest major general in the United States Armed Forces. He fought in the Battle of the Bulge, jumped out of planes as a paratrooper in the 82nd Airborne Division, and served in Korea and Vietnam. He flew over nine hundred combat missions (five times he was shot down by enemy fire), earning the nickname "Jumpin' Jack" and over forty decorations and citations for bravery, including three Purple Hearts. During the brief periods that he wasn't airborne, he managed to earn degrees from the University of Maryland, George Washington University, and Harvard.

Like her brother, Laverne fully assimilated her parents' work ethic and chronic fortitude. Now, surrounded by her daughters, Laverne sat upright, her snow white hair cropped and coifed, her face impassive, her demeanor composed even in the midst of devastation. Mimi did most of the talking. She told Laverne that I had colon cancer, but she remained intentionally hazy regarding the details. Our mother is vivacious—she lives on her own, drives around town, and attends more social functions than most people half her age—but still, she was almost ninety.

My mom had not cried when Mimi told her about my diagnosis. She was not a crier. Not at her husband's funeral several years before. Not now. Laverne had sat there, unmoving, quietly absorbing the impact of a cancer diagnosis. But when I walked into the room less than twenty minutes later, the forbearing exterior cracked. She began weeping. So did I.

"Why couldn't this have happened to me and not you?" she cried. Her voice was soft and faltering. "I've lived my life. It should be me. Not you."

There were more tears. Dave and I kept details at a minimum. We talked for thirty minutes. Maybe. It felt like an eternity.

Those were awful, awful conversations. But the hardest conversations came on Sunday, when we had to tell Kati and Kyle.

Kati was in the family room watching TV, surrounded by pillows, when Dave walked in.

"Hey, Kati."

She looked up.

"We need to talk to you."

Dave's tone was serious. Kati knew something was wrong. She thought she was in trouble. When I walked into the room, Kati was certain of it. She just didn't know why.

I started the conversation. At least, I tried, but the words wouldn't come. I looked at Kati. I looked at Dave.

"You know your mom had a colonoscopy the other day?" Dave stepped in.

"Yeah."

"They found some cancer."

"What are you talking about?" She was blindsided. "Is this a joke?"

No, this was not a joke, we said. But we had talked to several doctors. The cancer wasn't a death sentence. The tumors were operable. And I was strong. We had hope.

"We're going to get a game plan together," Dave told

her. "We don't know exactly how serious it is, but we're going to get a game plan."

"And, Kati, please don't Google it," I cautioned her.

But all Kati heard was noise. She was crying. I was crying. Dave was crying. I knew she would take it really hard, and she did. It was all too much for her. She didn't believe us. She was angry. She was sixteen.

Kati ran upstairs to her bedroom, locking the door behind her. Dave could hear her sobbing into her pillow as he knocked on the door. We still had to tell Kyle. We were going to call him now. We wanted Kati to be there, too, on the phone. He entreated her to unlock the door. But she didn't answer. Dave stood in the hallway, waiting for a response between the sobs, but Kati would remain in her room the rest of the night.

Six hundred miles away, Kyle was at Dave's brother Mark's home in Dallas. Kyle had transferred from Wake Forest and was now attending school at Dave's alma mater, SMU. He often visited his aunt and uncle on the weekends to watch football and enjoy a home-cooked meal. When Mark invited him over to watch the Cowboys' game, he figured it was just another Sunday in Dallas.

Mark and Peggy were in Mark's office when Kyle arrived. The three chatted for a while, but their small talk was interrupted when Chuck, who had flown in from St. Louis that morning, walked into the room. Peggy stood up and left the office as her brother-in-law sat down. Kyle suddenly felt uneasy.

His suspicions grew when his cell phone rang a few minutes later and the caller ID flashed Dave's name. He glanced up at Mark and Chuck as he answered. They had known we were going to call.

Kyle could tell we were upset even in the first few seconds. He immediately thought it was about my mom. He was certain she had passed away, and he waited for us to tell him the news.

"Kyle," Dave's voice came through the receiver. "We've got some bad news about mom."

He remained silent.

"Kyle," I said, "I have cancer."

Silence.

"What kind?" he finally said. "How bad is it?"

"It's not good," I replied. "It's stage IV."

I hadn't wanted to cry over the phone, but I couldn't help it. Kyle listened as we relayed the diagnosis, the statistics, the battle strategy. It was the same horrific story. Over and over. I could hear Kyle crying. Across the room, Mark was crying. So was Chuck. Kyle had never seen them cry before.

Like so many things in life, my relationship with Kyle had had its own set of struggles. But the prospect of permanent severance often has a way of mending lesser chasms, and it did so then.

"Mom, I'm sorry. I love you so much. I'm sorry for everything I've done."

"I forgive you. I'm sorry too. And I love you so much."

The call wasn't long. We said we loved each other, said we were going to get through this, said we loved each other again.

Mark and Chuck tried to reassure Kyle as he hung up the phone. They would be there for him. It was no coincidence that Kyle was in Texas at this point in his life, they said. They were going to support him through this. The three Griege men stood up, eyes red, and hugged. Then they left Mark's office.

As a preschooler at Visitation Academy

Dave and I during our dating years.

Dave and I married in 1987.

Dave, Kyle, Kati, and me in the late 1990s.

JoAnn, Mimi, Laverne, and me.

Bell-ringing ceremony at Siteman Cancer Center. Both JoAnn
and I had just completed major chemotherapy. Now it was time
for maintenance chemo.

Running under the St. Louis Arch, the Gateway to the West.

My army in Kona.

With my oncologist, Dr. Benjamin Tan,
who traveled to Kona to watch me compete. How cool is that?

A dream is realized: Crossing the finish line in Kona.

My wonderful family: Dave, Kyle, and Kati.

With Amy after the Undy 5000 for the Colon
Cancer Alliance. Awards time!

JoAnn, Laverne, Mimi, and me on the set of *The Ellen Degeneres Show.*

Dave and me with Chrissie Wellington in London.

With Dave after running the London Marathon.

* * *

"God wired us to need each other. We have in our DNA a need to connect with God. That same DNA created us to need each other from the very beginning. He made us relational."

Judy West's voice carried across the packed auditorium of The Crossing. With its modern lines and stadium seating, the room is more akin to a movie theater than a sanctuary. I sat in the dim light near the back. It was Saturday evening, two days after my diagnosis.

"God created people," she continued, "not a person in a vacuum, but people." Turning to the book of Genesis, she led the congregation through a brief recap of the creation account. God, at the end of each day of creation, assessed His work and found it to be good. The sun, moon, stars, plants, animals, mankind—all of creation—was good. Yet there was one thing that was not right. As Genesis 2:18 records: "The LORD God said, 'It is not good for man to be alone.'" If in a perfect world we were not meant to live in isolation, how much more in the hardships of life do we need the help of others?

Judy went on. "Life can get interesting. Life can get hard. Life can be a marathon. None of us were meant to go the distance alone."

I listened as the words cut through my situation. The message was direct. It was personal. I had never been one to want assistance. Yes, asking for help with my addictions had been a big step, but I didn't want to be a burden. I didn't want to make a big deal of my diagnosis. I could fight this on my own. I was strong. I was proud.

And then Judy told the story of Maria De Jesus and the Badwater Ultramarathon.

The Badwater Ultramarathon is a 135-mile race from Badwater in Death Valley in California to Mount Whitney. It is the most extreme and challenging footrace in the world.

Sunk into the earth at an abysmal 282 feet below sea level, the town of Badwater marks the lowest point in the Western Hemisphere. Average temperatures hover around 115 degrees Fahrenheit . . . at night. Midday, they soar above 130. Insipid and forsaken, the landscape is the dismal thumbprint of fire and brimstone, hell without the gates and pitchforks. Rising beyond the nebulous horizon, 8,500 feet above the desert floor, the hoary peaks of the Whitney Portals form a jagged skirt around Mount Whitney, the highest point in the contiguous United States. In their own saw-toothed way, the Whitney Portals are as unforgiving as the valley below, their cruelty incarnated in long, soul-crushing ascents and volatile conditions.

The path between the two extremes is blurred and ghostlike in the haze that rises from the pavement and melts the monochromatic vista like watercolors. The road is desolate, the land startlingly uninhabitable. It is the perfect setting for phantasmagoria and the worst place imaginable for an ultramarathon. Yet that is exactly what it is.

Participants are allowed up to two support vans for supplies, but they must run on their own volition, without physical assistance, cooling vests, or IV fluids—all of which result in disqualification. They drape themselves head to toe in white in desperate attempts to deflect as much heat as possible. They run on the white line stretching down the road, like tightrope walkers rehearsing at ground level, keeping their feet on the paint so the soles of their shoes don't melt on the pavement. They run by towns and landmarks with names like Devil's Cornfield and Furnace Creek. And in addition to dehydration, cramping, vomiting, swelling, and blisters—those are just par for the course—they face the very real threats of organ failure and brain damage. To top things off, they have to complete the distance in under sixty hours. A third of those who start the race never see the finish line.

Yet incredibly, each year, just shy of one hundred participants from around the globe accept the Badwater challenge. Maria De Jesus, an ultramarathoner from Great Britain, was one of them.

Maria was what Judy called a "lone ranger." She had no family or friends able to travel with her to California as her support crew. She took out a bank loan to pay her way to the race and sent word to the U.S. that she was looking for someone willing to drive her support van. A sympathetic stranger answered her request for help. The two met for the first time at the airport, shook hands, and headed to Badwater. This man whom Maria had met only hours before would be responsible for all of her gear, food, water, hydration, and medical and emotional needs. He was, in essence, responsible for her life.

One hundred miles into the race, Maria collapsed. Bleeding, blistered, dehydrated, and on the verge of delirium, she crawled into the van. Her sidekick, the good but fatigued Samaritan, had fallen asleep at the wheel—literally. Maria lay in the desperate solitude of her van, emotionally and physically annihilated. She knew her race was coming to an end.

Meanwhile, forty miles behind her, a U.S. Marine out of Camp Pendleton, California, had already seen the end of his. He had trained for the race for months and had gathered a coterie of fellow Marines to be his support crew. But the distance and conditions can decimate even the best prepared. At mile sixty, his body shut down. His team had to carry him on a makeshift stretcher so he could receive medical aid and IV fluids, which simultaneously saved his life and disqualified him from the contest. With their buddy out of the race, the Marines heard about Maria's situation and decided they would find her. They would be her support crew.

Maria lay crumpled and defeated in her van when the Marines arrived. They were there for her, they said. They would help her reach the end. She was not alone.

Bolstered by their encouragement, defying physiological impossibilities and a body that only moments before had been shutting down, Maria got up and began running. She ran the final thirty-five miles of the race surrounded by a sea of soldiers, crossing the finish line in forty-three hours.

Images of Maria at the finish flashed across the projector screen hanging above the stage where Judy spoke.

"Some of you are sitting here saying, 'I feel alone.' Well, do something. Say something." She smiled. "Maybe it's time to call in the Marines."

The congregation bowed their heads in prayer, and the service ended.

I lay awake in bed that night, unable to sleep. The story of Maria De Jesus replayed itself in my head. I knew the message had been for me. I was supposed to hear it. I had needed to hear it. And now it was time to take action.

I would form an army.

8

THE BATTLE BEGINS

I officially declared war on Tuesday, September 22, five days after my diagnosis. The clandestine communications of the previous days had finally come to an end. I spent the day at Barnes-Jewish Hospital West County, a branch of "Big Barnes" downtown. My niece Julie continued to orchestrate my meetings with doctors and surgeons, and by the time I woke up on Tuesday morning, I had a litany of appointments.

The first set of meetings took place at the Siteman Cancer Center, a pale-brown brick building perched adjacent to the main hospital in the Barnes West complex just south of Olive Boulevard. I made my way through the sliding glass doors for what would be the first of hundreds of visits, visits that would punctuate my days and weeks from that point on. From the moment Dave and I arrived at the hospital, my niece Julie acted as our personal escort, shepherding us from one appointment to the next. At that point, everything was still a blur. Having Julie there to guide us through the entire process, literally arm-in-arm, provided immeasurable reassurance.

The opening ceremonies began with the radiation oncologist. It was a relay of introduction, communication, and examination as I was passed from one specialist to the next. At each stop, I had to endure the inglorious procedure of a rectal exam. Everybody poked up my butt that day. Colon cancer is very humbling.

By the end of the afternoon, the Siteman crew had outlined my plan of care, from radiation to chemo to surgery. Their first offensive would begin the following Monday: I would receive a week of radiation, take the next week off, and then start chemo.

After all the appointments were over, Dave and I returned to the main Siteman building for a final chat with Dr. Tan, my medical oncologist. Dave had one more question. It didn't have to do with cancer. It had to do with Hawaii.

Earlier in the year, Scott Stern had applied for a lottery slot in the Ironman World Championship. Of the eighteen hundred athlete spots, sixteen hundred are awarded through qualification. The rest are reserved for lottery, giving those who cannot qualify by time a chance to compete on the sacred ground of Kona. Scott had been one such applicant, and his name had been drawn from the proverbial hat. Dave and I wanted to be there to cheer him on.

Dave asked Dr. Tan if the trip was still possible. The race was at the beginning of October, less than two weeks away. Could I go to Kona and then start chemo when I returned? The delay would be only a couple of days. Dr. Tan gave his blessing, and the amendment was made. Finally, we headed home.

The call to arms went out that night. A close family friend, Tommye Fleming, volunteered to be my "Army Recruiter" and began the draft. She created a blog for me on CaringBridge, an online resource for people battling serious illnesses. Through the blog, I could easily keep family and friends informed of my progress; in response, they could send messages of encouragement. I wrote my first post that evening, asking for soldiers to join my army. The response was immediate and overwhelming. Relatives, friends, training buddies, simple acquaintances—even people whom I had never before met—began enlisting, choosing their service and position. Dave was the commander in chief. He led the charge with unwavering strength, and his quiet confidence was a pillar of strength for me. My niece Julie, who had coordinated all of my appointments at Barnes, would be the general. Cristel, true to her fiery personality, declared herself a sniper so she could be "on the front lines." Most people joined as foot soldiers, ready for ground fighting. Within hours of the first post, the ranks filled up.

Your 4-star general here! Sending you all my love and prayers. Your courage is an inspiration. I have been keeping your chart up to date on my end and you know that I will command everything to be done in a timely fashion, as any good general should! XOXO!

—General Julie Wilson

We are here for you. Day or night. I will respect your right to talk about cancer when you want to, not when I think I need to know. We need to ride, run, and keep you as fit as possible so your body fights and recovers quickly.

—Cristel Santiago
Sniper
Teri's Army

My niece Christi, with whom I had trained for the Chicago marathon, was also one of the first to join:

T,
You are my mentor, my friend, my cohort in crime, my sunshine, my inspiration on so many levels, and you are my aunt. I will lead your charge, along with those who love you, and

we will only LOOK FORWARD. "He lifts you up
and turns you around and puts your feet back
on solid ground."

Love Always,
Chris [Christi] Liebe

. . . As was my sister-in-law Jessica, Chuck's wife:

Hey Ter,
Chuck and I are suited up and ready to go
alongside you in battle—and so are [our] 3
little soldiers!

Love,
Jess and Chuck and the kids

The messages poured in by the hundreds. Family and friends
drafted their own family and friends, who in turn did the
same. Soldiers emerged from our current neighborhood,
our old neighborhood, our church, my gym, my spin classes,
and my swim clubs. They came marching from the triathlon
community and the cycling community, from Greenbriar
and from AA. They came from my high school and my kids'
schools—friends, parents, and teachers. Larger and larger the
army grew. My girlfriends from real estate. Dave's work associ-
ates. Dave's siblings even drafted members of their churches
and prayer groups in Dallas, and I often received emails from

total strangers hundreds of miles away, strangers who were praying for me, who were in my army. One email I received was from a young Marine stationed overseas. Although we had never met, he wanted me to know that I had a Marine in my battalion. People supplied meals, which was a double blessing, since Dave and Kati are always relieved when they don't have to eat my cooking. (To be fair, anyone would be relieved that they don't have to eat my cooking.) They brought gifts, offered rides, volunteered time, wrote missives of encouragement, and extended thoughts and prayers. My post had been a rally cry, and the citizenry had responded in a viral phenomenon.

Have already recruited my Bible study to be in your army. Also, have many other friends who are already praying for you. I am available to drive to treatments, provide meals, pray, talk, or just sit with you. Most of all, you have my love. God bless you and give you stamina as you fight this fight. Also, may He work through your doctors to heal you.

In Him,
—Kathy Fullerton

All my thoughts and prayers are with you. I am letting all my prayer warrior friends know that there is a battle to be fought, and you can trust that you are being lifted up in prayer on [a] daily basis. We are here for you and love you.

—Laurie Smith

Sign me up, I'm in and I'm with you. You are awesome, Teri. You amaze me with your ironman races and inspire me with [your] devotion to God. Get some good doctors and [a lot] of prayers and we'll kick this thing.

Love,
Kelly Main

My niece Julie's high school friend Liz wrote:

After all these years I truly think of you as my own "Aunt TT" and that comes with a whole heart full of love for you and the rest of my Fabulous Francisco Girls. As a person who has had her share of nasty life moments I know a person with a warrior spirit when I see it. You got it in spades, girl! And you have the unlimited strength of God at your complete disposal. Jesus, though a man of peace, was a warrior of the soul and he will see you through. So let it rip, my sweet!

All My Love,
Liz [Elizabeth] Snyder

Many of the messages began with introductions as I met my soldiers for the first time over the CaringBridge guestbook:

> We have never met but I am a swimming friend of Lori Payne. She told me about your health problems. You and your family are and always [will] be in my prayers. You will fight this [demon] and you will win. Thanks for putting up this site to keep us all informed on your progress.
>
> —Janet Criscione

> We have not met, but I am a lifelong friend of Jessica. I want you to know that my prayers and thoughts will be with you daily. How honored I am to be a soldier with you.
>
> —Michelle Johnson

Others were spiced with humor:

> Good luck today, my friend! And you SHOULD be a hugger—a minimum of three hugs a day is recommended (really) because it increases hemoglobins or something. My dad told me that when I was little and I'm sure he wouldn't lie about something so important. Can I be on

the SWAT team? I like swatting things. And certain people.

Love,
Becky Kling

If you think medals for finishing the Ironman are cool, wait until you see the one for beating this. You're in my prayers. Also, I think you get a t-shirt too!

—Marc Campbell

Just wanted to say hi to my training buddy and fieldtrip companion. We've pedaled many miles together, laughed and cried and maybe even changed a flat . . . No, I don't think we ever had a flat........ Crash, yes. Flat, no. How about that! In 23 years of racing a bike, Teri is one of the best training partners I have had. Not only does she push you competitively, but the miles just click away easily and nothing is ever a problem. Just a wonderful, happy friend. Thank you, TT.

Col. PJ
Special Forces/Covert Operations

Kati and her friends also contributed to the guestbook:

Hey Mrs. Griege (: I really like this caring bridge thing, and want you to know I love you, and pray for you everyday. I know you can do it (: love, lucy devereux

Hii mommy :) I hope u have a fabulous time on your trip! I'll miss you!! MWAH! Love your BB4L (you know what it means hehe) I love you, silly!

katiloulou

My great-nephew Jack, Courtney's son and an eight-year-old of few words, kept things to the point:

"GO T.T. GO"

One message would prove to be particularly prophetic, though I didn't know it at the time:

You have a new 'ironman' to achieve this year and I have no doubt that in 2011 you will be celebrating your 50th participating in the Ironman in Hawaii.

All my well wishes and prayers are sent your way!

—Jeannette French

I was prepped for radiation and chemotherapy on September 23. ("So today was a long and busy day—again," I wrote on my blog. "Went down to Barnes and had a port inserted for chemotherapy. I also was marked for radiation therapy ... The next few days I hope to catch my breath and of course exercise . . .") My lower abdomen was tattooed with ink dots marking the exact area to receive radiation and ensuring exact precision in the daily treatments. (Tattoo being the operative word: while radiation markings are small, they are also permanent.) And a port was implanted beneath the skin just below my right shoulder, serving as an access point for intravenous chemo. I was fully accessorized and ready for treatment.

Sunday, September 27, 2009

It is Sunday night and tomorrow the ground war begins. Radiation treatment #1. I am ready. Trained 50 miles on my bike today with two of my favorite riding buddies. What a beautiful day to be outside. Good to feel the sun. I still at times [cannot] believe I am sick if I feel sooo good and can do sooo much. Go figure!

Kyle headed back to Dallas. We had a
great visit. I already miss him and I know Kati
does too.

I hope everyone had a great weekend.
I enlisted a number of personnel over the past
few days—special forces, navy seal, swat,
lots of foot soldiers, and a few snipers too.

Hugs (I guess I am a hugger now),
Teri

Radiation was a five-day offensive. Dave went with me. The
treatment itself took thirty minutes, most of which was spent
double-checking measurements.

They gave [Dave] a tour of the room and equipment. All in a good day. The rest of the week
the treatments will take place at 1:30 p.m. That
way I can get some training in before I report.
Tomorrow I am going to go swim with my masters group. They wear me out—I can't wait.

Battle on my friends
—Teri

Two days after my first radiation treatment, I signed up for the
2010 Ironman Branson 70.3. It was a September event, exactly
a year away. I marked it on my calendar. ("… I stopped by the

bike shop (Ghisallo) today and got a warm welcome," I wrote. "Thanks guys. Dave was relieved I did not come home with another new bike. Little does he know I have picked out my next race!")

Not training was never an option. From the moment I was diagnosed, I knew I would keep racing and competing. Ruben had planted the seed when he compared my battle to a full Ironman. This was an endurance event. I would attack this situation with the same determination and staying power I used in training and racing. I wasn't going to throw a pity party. I wasn't going to succumb to morbidity. I would not let the disease beat me. Cancer would not determine my existence.

And so, the day I was diagnosed, I made Ironman Branson 70.3 my goal race. I knew I had to put a goal out there. You can always change your goal, but if you don't sign up and make it real, you've got nothing to reach for. Having a goal gives you a sense of control. For me, signing up for Branson was like saying, "I'm beating cancer. This cancer isn't beating me."

Dave and I said, "Okay, fine. I've got cancer. Let's get after it." There was still life to be lived. This was no time to sit around and mope. We determined to enjoy the day and enjoy our lives and not play the "What If" game. We were going to keep pressing forward. We were going to be positive about the whole situation. We didn't know how long I had left to live—two years, five years, whatever. The only thing we did know was that we weren't going to stop living our lives to the fullest.

Thursday, October 1, 2009

A short story to tell. Last week down at Big Barnes, Mimi and I were waiting in the oncology dept. All of [a] sudden we see a man walk over to a bell that is hanging on the wall. He rings it—and it is loud. Then all the people in the area clap their hands, so we join in. Come to find out a person gets to ring the bell when they have completed their last radiation treatment.

I am receiving all of my radiation treatments at Barnes West. This is a brand new facility so they just had their bell installed. When I arrived today the radiation techs were very proud to inform me that tomorrow I will be the first patient to ring the bell. How cool is that! Many mixed emotions . . .

On Friday, I received my last radiation treatment. Mimi went with me. I walked out of the treatment room only to discover a contingent of my army waiting by the bell: Dave, my mom, my nieces, and my grandnieces and grandnephews. They were all dressed in yellow Livestrong T-shirts. I rang the bell as the army cheered.

Let's just say it was an incredible moment. Above the bell is a plaque and on it inscribed— "Life is not measured by the number of breaths we take, but by the moments that take our breath away. Smile—this is one of those moments."

It certainly was one of those moments—tears and smiles.

Later in the day was the Livestrong celebration, which included a bike ride and dinner. It was so much fun and a big success. Thank you to all who came and supported the event.

Kati had homecoming this weekend. Her class won the spirit award. She was very excited about that. She looked so beautiful in her homecoming dress!! I had a great time taking pictures before the dance.

It is hard to describe the emotions of Friday. It was a very special day. What I considered an accomplishment is very different from what I now consider an accomplishment. . . .

Dave and I left for Hawaii the following week. Jeff and Trish Eddy also made the trip. We, along with a contingent of family and friends, would be Scott's support group.

Scott was as prepared and fit as he had ever been. To ready his body for the Kona heat, he would haul his bike into his garage on the hottest summer afternoons, close the garage door, and knock out a multi-hour ride in the stifling air. But the conditions in Kona, infamously brutal, were vengeful in 2009, with temperatures rising into the upper nineties and extreme humidity that sent the heat index soaring. The race was a struggle. After the swim, he forgot to apply sunscreen. By the end of the bike, he was so burned that his race number, 967, was permanently seared onto his arm. (Though the "9" is fading, the "67" is still clearly visible today.) The run wasn't much better. In his previous two Ironmans, Scott had run every mile of the marathon leg. In Kona, he was on the marathon course all of ten feet before he started walking. Dave ran and walked Palani hill with Scott, encouraging him to take his time, directing him to put one foot in front of the other, letting him know that he had family and friends there to support him. Sixteen miles later, Scott crossed the finish line of a race he had always dreamed of doing. But the race had proved to be a traitorous lover.

The beauty of Kona can be cruel, masking the struggles of those who cross its Mata Hari landscape. For Scott, the deception revealed itself on race morning. For me, it occurred the night before.

We were all out to dinner the evening before the race—nearly twenty of us crowded around the table. My phone rang in the middle of the meal. It was my niece Julie. I excused myself and stepped outside. Dave followed.

"Hey, Julie. What's going on?"

Something was up. Julie wouldn't call unless she had something important to report, something that couldn't wait. I looked at my watch. A five-hour time difference meant it was late in St. Louis.

"Teri," Julie said, her voice low and factual. "JoAnn's biopsy came back positive. She has cancer."

9

JOANN

===========================

"I'm not going to drink that stuff and then poop in the doctor's office."

JoAnn was adamant. She had no risk factors for colon cancer and, until I was diagnosed, no family history of cancer at all. She was fit. She was healthy. She had no symptoms. Plus, this was no time to be thinking about herself. I was the sick one. Lightning wasn't going to strike our family twice.

"You're sixty-two, and you've never had a colonoscopy."

JoAnn's husband, Chuck, had fought this battle before. JoAnn hated going to the doctor. Hated it. And so, to Chuck's chagrin, she never did. For the most part, Chuck didn't press

the issue—not that it would have made a difference—though
he did ask that she get a checkup on her fiftieth birthday. She
agreed. That was in 1998. Before that, her last doctor's visit
was in 1983.

"Listen, there are only two things that are gonna get
me: Alzheimer's or a car wreck."

"JoAnn."

She shook her head. "No."

"Yes, you have to do this."

"No, I don't. I will not."

But Chuck had had enough. "Oh, yes, you will."

Chuck scheduled the procedure despite JoAnn's
remonstrance. He bought the preparation supplies—including
a giant jug of chalky white bowel cleanser, which he very nearly
had to pour down her throat. She thought it was all a big waste
of time, but if it would make everyone happy—if it would
finally get Chuck off her back—well, then, she'd do it.

"A car wreck or Alzheimer's, Chuck. But not cancer.
I'm impervious to cancer."

JoAnn had maintained an impressive image from
the time she first graced the formerly cloistered halls of
Visitation Academy. She looked, dressed, and acted older
than she was, so much so that even as a young child people
designated her an "old soul." When she was seven, she had
the foresight to accept her aunt's offer to see an emerging
rock and roll star and ended up front row center watching Elvis Presley. By the time she was thirteen, she was
going on "car dates" with boys who were old enough to pick
her up from our parents' house. She began dating Chuck
at the tender age of fourteen. She was the prom queen at
fifteen. After high school, she attended St. Louis University,

graduating magnum cum laude in six semesters. She got married ten days later. She was twenty.

JoAnn hated sports and really any activity that required exertion or caused her to sweat. To her credit, she gave aerobics a whirl when she was thirty, after two kids and Jane Fonda convinced her a little exercise might be beneficial. She liked it so much she decided to become an aerobics instructor, pioneering the 1980s neon fling with Lycra and leg warmers. Thirty years later, she was still teaching students the grapevine at the gym where she worked.

At sixty-one, JoAnn was as fit, lean, and stylish as ever. A healthy diet and multiple workouts per week (and sometimes per day) kept her figure svelte and tone. Her smooth, blonde hair graced her shoulders and framed the string of pearls that was inevitably around her neck. She wore her jeans skinny and her rings diamond. And without earrings, well, she may as well have been naked (at least in her mind). The idea of a colonoscopy, then, was utterly distasteful, quite literally when you consider she had to drink a gallon of unpalatably chalky polyethylene glycol in lieu of the "dynamite pills" that I took. The sooner the whole ordeal was over, the better. She would go in, get screened, and go home. It would all be very simple and very quick. Or so she thought.

JoAnn was just waking up from the anesthesia when the doctor walked into the recovery room.

"You have a very large tumor in your cecum," he said without ceremony, slinging his hand with routine apathy in the direction of a shadowy blob on an illuminated x-ray screen. "I've looked at it. I've poked it. I can guarantee you it's not cancer."

JoAnn stared at the x-ray. She was still groggy.

"It's just a cyst. I'm going to send you to the surgeon. You'll make an appointment. You'll have it taken out." He was curt. There was no intent to comfort. "Again, I can guarantee you it is not cancer."

Ten days later, JoAnn had colon resection surgery. She wasn't nervous. Even when she scheduled the operation, the colon surgeon had reassured her the tumor was benign.

"I know your doctor," he said. "He wouldn't say it wasn't cancer if he didn't know for certain that it wasn't cancer. Trust what he says. He's been doing this for twenty years, and he's seen a lot of tumors."

Julie made the trip from St. Louis to Columbia and stayed with JoAnn while she recovered. The surgery was a roaring success—as much as slicing into a human body can be. The surgeons removed all of JoAnn's ascending colon and over half of her transverse colon. They found a seed tumor in one of her lymph nodes and, as a precaution, removed the rest of the lymph nodes in the area. The specimens were sent to pathology for testing. Meanwhile, JoAnn recovered in record time. The surgery was on Wednesday; by Friday, she was able to eat and, to the astonishment of the hospital staff, have regular bowel movements. She was cleared for release on Saturday morning. Her overnight stay on Friday would be mere formality. Plus, they were still awaiting results from pathology. Official results, anyway. The surgeon had seen the tumor, felt the tumor, removed the tumor. It was not cancerous.

JoAnn was talking to Julie when the doctor walked into her room. They could tell by the look on his face that whatever he had to say wasn't good.

The giant tumor was benign. But nestled inside the large tumor was a smaller tumor. The smaller tumor was cancerous. So was the seed tumor in the lymph node. He wanted a CT scan of her abdomen to see if the cancer had spread to any of the surrounding organs. It was at least stage III. Only further tests would show if it were worse.

Julie immediately called Chuck. He had just left the hospital to spend a few hours at their grandson's baseball party. She also demanded that her mom go to "Big Barnes" for her scans as soon as she recovered enough to make the drive to St. Louis. Big Barnes had the newest, most advanced equipment. The accuracy of the CT scans and MRIs impact survival. There is a critical difference between stage III and stage IV colon cancer. The former is beatable. The latter may not be.

Meanwhile, JoAnn sat in silence. She was convinced that she had been misdiagnosed, that the pathology results were erroneous or that somehow the department had messed up. Even when Chuck arrived and everybody started hugging and crying and talking about what they would do next, JoAnn refused to believe the diagnosis. After all, she was impervious to cancer. And even if the tumors had been cancerous, they were already out of her body, weren't they? Everything would be fine. She was fine. She truly believed the whole thing was some terrible mistake.

On Saturday, I called JoAnn from Hawaii. Julie had told me the news the night before. She had also sent JoAnn's CT scans to Big Barnes. The radiologist said the spots on her liver looked suspect. JoAnn would head to St. Louis after a couple of days for another set of scans and her final diagnosis.

Separated by four thousand miles, JoAnn and I had a poignant and intimate conversation. We talked about finding out we had cancer, about accepting it, about anger, about fear, about grief, about surviving, about dying.

"Do you ever wake up crying in the middle of the night?" JoAnn asked.

"Yeah. That first week . . ." I paused. "I cried myself to sleep every night that week. Quietly, you know? I'd just find myself crying. I don't know . . . in the middle of the night, the reality hits you. I'd just lie there and think about the reality of not being there anymore."

For a moment, we were quiet.

"Won't it be awful if one of us makes it and one of us doesn't?" I asked.

JoAnn told me later that part of her wished it had been stage IV. All she could think was, "How am I going to live if Teri dies?" She viewed it as though I saved her life. There is no way to describe what it feels like when you are faced with your own mortality. You feel sorry for yourself. You feel sorry for the people you love. And then you feel sorry for yourself again. It is a very strange jumble of emotions.

As it had with me, the reality of the diagnosis hit JoAnn the hardest at night. She'd wake up in the middle of the night to find her pillow wet with tears and her eyes swollen. In the middle of the night, she realized she could be dying. In the middle of the night, she realized she could be gone within a few years. Or within a few months. She thought about Chuck. She thought about her daughters, Julie and Cary. She thought about her grandkids and how she wouldn't get to see them play summer baseball or graduate from high school or go off to college or get married. She'd cry herself back to sleep and then, when morning came, she'd return to stubborn disbelief. The whole thing was some terrible mistake.

A week after her diagnosis, JoAnn had recovered enough to travel to St. Louis. Once more, my niece Julie took command, setting up JoAnn's appointment with one of the top radiologists at Barnes—the same radiologist who had looked at my scans. In addition to scheduling another CT scan and MRI, Julie arranged to have JoAnn's blood work redone. As she had done in my situation, Julie labored to expedite her mom's tests and appointments. Without Julie's orchestration, the whole process would have taken much longer. JoAnn and I were greatly indebted to her.

Twenty minutes after JoAnn's tests were completed, they had their answer. The spots on her liver were benign fat cysts. They were common and harmless. The disease had not metastasized to any other part of her abdomen. The cancer was not stage IV.

By the time JoAnn and Chuck finally pulled into the garage of their home in Columbia, the strain of the past week had taken its toll on JoAnn. The anxiety of not knowing her full diagnosis, the discomfort of fasting for and enduring a never-ending series of tests, and the confusing emotional burden of dealing with stage III cancer even as she absorbed the truth of my stage IV diagnosis—all while recovering from major surgery, no less—proved to be too much. Yes, she was relieved her cancer hadn't yet advanced to its worst stage. Yes, stage III was beatable. And yes, she had already had the tumors removed. But she wasn't in the clear yet. She would need chemo. A lot of it. Between her own treatment and mine, cancer would dominate JoAnn's life for the foreseeable future.

10

TRAINING, TREATMENT AND FANNY

Thursday, October 15, 2009

Well, in just a few hours phase 2 of the ground war begins. If all goes according to plan I will begin my first round of chemotherapy. Not exactly sure what to expect. I think I will be at the hospital for 6 hours or so while they begin the treatment. Then I come home with an infusion pump for about 48 hours. I will let you know how it goes . . .

. . . I am up late for a few reasons. First

it is about 7 p.m. Hawaii time and second I am having a hard time sleeping. This past week our family again has been given some tragic news. My sister JoAnn (who lives in Columbia, MO) has also been [diagnosed] with colon cancer. So far we know there is lymph node involvement and are awaiting further [tests] on the liver and lungs. I have no words— I do not know what to say. Can this really be happening?!!

So—I am calling in all the troops for backup.

It looks like we have another soldier to support.

Please [pray] for JoAnn and our family as we try to make our way through this most difficult time. Hopefully we will know more tomorrow.

One day at a time,
Teri

JoAnn returned to St. Louis to see Dr. Tan, my oncologist. JoAnn would need twelve rounds of chemo—a minimum of six months of treatment if there were no complications, longer if her body couldn't recover on schedule. But there was a setback right out of the gate. The results of JoAnn's blood work revealed that the tumors had caused internal bleeding; for months her body had been stealthily absorbing the blood. As a result, her iron counts were low—far too low to begin chemotherapy. She would need an iron infusion before she could withstand chemo. She scheduled her infusion for the day of my first chemo treatment. JoAnn would receive chemotherapy in Columbia, but at least for this first step in her own treatment and this watershed in my own, we would be together.

Mimi went with us to Barnes West. So did our mom. We were led into a large square room lined with windows and vinyl recliners accessorized with silver IV poles and hanging bags of medicine. I took a seat in one of the large treatment chairs. A nurse hooked me up to an IV, and the first round of chemo began pumping its way into my body. JoAnn was placed next to me in an identical chair complete with the same blinking and beeping IV paraphernalia. Two waiting room chairs were solicited for Mimi and our mom.

Before long, Dr. Tan walked into the room. With his soft, Filipino accent he spoke with JoAnn and me and talked about our treatment. Mimi, the acting supervisor, asked questions and took notes.

But my mom had grown quiet. She sat between JoAnn and me, holding our hands while the clicking of the IVs ticked away the seconds. The treatment room was a study in survival. Some patients were my age. Some were much older. Some were covered in blankets. Some were talking quietly to family members. Some were sleeping. Some looked relatively healthy. Many did not. All looked battle weary. The war against cancer is cruel; the disease and the treatment advance with merciless aggression, and the body is sacrificed in the crossfire.

Finally, Laverne looked at us again, her two youngest daughters. Tubes protruded from our chests. White medical tags shackled our wrists. We were young. We had families. It was all too terrible for her to handle. She began crying.

Dr. Tan stopped talking. He looked at our mom and her crown of smooth white hair and deep brown eyes that had just as much luster as they did when she was a young girl. Now they were filled with tears. He walked over to where she sat between us. He lowered himself to his knees and took both of her hands in his own. Now at eye level with the brokenhearted mother, Dr. Tan spoke with quiet, determined compassion.

"Don't worry, Laverne," he said. "I'm going to take good care of both of your girls."

I reported on CaringBridge later that evening:

> . . . Today was a loooong day. We were at the hospital (Barnes West) for about 6 hours. All went well and I came home with my infusion pump in a fine looking fanny pack. I am thinking it needs some bling—black is boring. This will be attached (the chemo infusing) till about noon on Sat. Then free again. Only side effect is cold—cold anything! Zero tolerance—and I am always cold anyway. Thinking swimming might be out for a while or maybe not. I miss the swim girls. O.K. I miss all my girlfriends. I am going to ride my bike indoor on the trainer tomorrow— boring, but at least I can do that. It is the little things in life . . .

"Fanny," as I affectionately dubbed my new fanny pack, would be a caddy for my chemotherapy treatment. I would get to know Fanny well, although efforts to give Fanny a makeover never quite panned out. (My nieces tried to put some bling on her, but it didn't stick. She remained Plain Jane Fanny.) I was scheduled for twelve rounds of chemotherapy: five rounds before surgery and seven rounds after. Every other Tuesday, I'd advance through a series of checks-ups, hallways, rooms, and more rooms. Because of the sheer efficiency and systematization of the whole process, the progression through the center hints of an assembly line of sorts. It's almost like you're in the future—all the chairs lined up, filled with people getting treated for cancer. It seems like it would be cold and mechanized, but somehow it's not. The staff sees to that.

While the term "chemo" is tossed around with homogeneous implications, the pharmaceuticals constituting each patient's treatment are not the same. Different cancers require different medicines, doses, and combinations; identical cancers may require unique treatment depending on the patient's needs and the plan of care selected by the oncologist.

Dr. Tan placed me on FOLFOX, a standard chemotherapy medicine used in the treatment of colon cancer, and Avastin, a drug that specifically targets tumors. It was a therapy combination designed to attack colon cancer from several angles. Cancer cells divide and spread rapidly, forming tumors. As the tumors grow, they need an increasing blood supply to survive. The tumors summon nearby blood vessels, using certain proteins as messengers. One such protein, vascular endothelial growth factor, or VEGF, issues a particularly emphatic subpoena. The acquiescent blood vessels follow the VEGF instructions and grow toward the tumor, providing a healthy and life-giving blood supply. FOLFOX is a combination of several drugs: 5-FU and oxaliplatin, both of which prevent cancer cells from proliferating, and leucovorin, which is used to increase the efficiency of the 5-FU. Avastin is an anti-angiogenic, or "tumor starving," drug that blocks VEGF from reaching the blood vessels, in effect cutting off the tumor's food supply. Working together, the two drugs blitz both the tumor and the blood vessels feeding the tumor. And most likely, Dr. Tan assured me, neither of them would make me lose my hair.

I received the chemo combo every other week, allowing one week between treatments for my body to recover. My initial treatments lasted five hours. Following the nurse into the treatment room, I would obediently take my seat in one of the patient chairs—a plump plastic recliner that didn't so much recline as give the appearance of being able to do so should the whim strike—while the nurse hooked me up to the IV. Dave would leave work to come sit with me and Mimi. He always picked up lunch on the way over—usually St. Louis Bread Company, a local bakery and café with excellent chocolate chip cookies—and we would have a little feast in the treatment room.

After I was exonerated from IV incarceration, I was sent home with Fanny—essentially house arrest—for two more days of intravenous treatment. For forty-eight hours, Fanny and I were inseparable. ("Dave took Fanny . . . and me to the movies last night," I recorded in my journal. "We saw *Couples Retreat* thinking some laughter would do us good . . .") Once I was unhooked from the bag, however, there was no love lost, and I would often celebrate my independence by shoving Fanny in a closet and promptly heading out for a run. ("The nurse came by about 11 a.m. and unhooked me—" I continued, "watch out, I am a free woman again. Heading out for a workout!!")

* * *

I continued training while receiving chemotherapy and radiation. I was given clearance from Dr. Tan and his nurse practitioner, Beth; although considering I was the first Ironman the staff had ever worked with, information was undoubtedly lost in translation. When I asked them about working out, they responded with affirmation. They had had patients walk on the treadmill before. But whether or not they realized that when I asked if I could "go for a run" I meant ten miles or that my "bike rides" were fifty-mile journeys is up for debate. But they never told me I couldn't.

I hopped in the pool when I could, though my swim sessions were less frequent than I would have preferred. When I was liberated from IV infusion, I'd throw on my running shoes and chalk off eight, nine, ten miles, often right from Siteman. But it was my bike rides with Fanny that freaked everybody out the most. The unpretentious little bag was accessorized with a clear, thin tube that snaked its way to a small port implanted under my skin where the chemo could be delivered intravenously. Riding my bike trainer was the one thing I could do while connected to a bag of poison. I simply plopped Fanny on a barstool next to my trainer in the basement, climbed on the bike, and pedaled for the next two or three hours. Most of the time I'd watch *Biggest Loser* or *The Ellen DeGeneres Show* while I rode. The whole thing—Fanny, the trainer, half-century rides—seemed natural. It wasn't that big of a deal. But to everyone else, the spectacle of me hunched over the handlebars and the clear tube protruding from my chest to the black bag deposited ingloriously on a barstool next to me, was relatively shocking.

But the hardest days of training through chemo weren't when my body physically wouldn't let me do what I wanted to do. Most of the time, I'd get in the miles I wanted—it would just take a long, long time. The worst days were the days when I would go in for chemo, and treatment would have to be delayed a week because my white blood counts were too low. I hated the delays in treatment. Delays pushed the finish line further back. I wanted to move forward with treatment, but the white blood count was out of my control. It was very difficult.

"Well round three has been delayed until next Tuesday," I wrote after one such day. "My white blood cells and neutophils were [too] low for me to receive the chemo. Basically they could not suppress my immune system any further. To say I was disappointed is an understatement. . . . So we won't be back in business until next week. I am praying for patience and acceptance. There is always so much to learn . . ."

Monday, October 19, 2009

I have to admit the last few days have been a little tougher. Life has slowed down and physically I haven't felt 100%, thus giving me time to be a little weaker. I need to get out of my head, pray, and stay positive, and not let fear [creep] in. I am sure I will get more comfortable with this down time between chemo treatments. It is just very hard to stay patient and not want to be so [proactive] all the time . . .

Monday, October 26, 2009

. . . Have done some biking and running (so miss the swimming) over the past few days. I realize my energy level will decrease for a little bit and I will probably be somewhat restless. It helps to have an idea of what is coming . . .

Saturday, October 31, 2009

. . . Went swimming Friday for the first time in three weeks. Felt great to be back in the water but was shocked at how quickly one can lose their conditioning . . . [B]ouncing back from chemo on Thursday. My Mom said something to me today that really hit home—"When you feel bad that must mean the medicine is working and working hard." For some reason that brought me comfort. Thanks Mom.

But despite setbacks, I knew I had to stay positive. I pushed through the difficult days and basked in the moments when the wind was at my back, firmly believing that every struggle would be counterbalanced by reward. Cancer increased my awareness of the present, and I found myself delighting in what before I took for granted. Every day I found new things for which to be grateful. Every day I found that being thankful made me strong.

Monday, November 9, 2009

. . . Just want to thank everyone. I truly believe I am doing so well because you all are carrying me through this—onward!

Friday, November 13, 2009

. . . Once again—Thanks. I feel like a broken record. Every [day] that goes by I am truly filled with gratitude for all the prayers and support.

Sunday, November 22, 2009

Well, it has been a while. Many times I don't feel like I have much to say or at least much worth saying. But, then I bump into someone and they tell me they find the updates helpful and sometimes even inspiring. I have never thought of myself in that light. The fact that I am able to comprise a message is a miracle! So, in a way, a new gift is revealed to me through this disease. I have received the gift of "awareness." One thing I do know is I have an acute awareness and appreciation of the present, the here and now . . .

Monday, November 23, 2009

[Every day] I think this will be the last beautiful day. Not a very good attitude. How quick that attitude of gratitude slips away, and the negative thinking seeps in!!

Well, I said each day I would list some things I am grateful for—so here it goes.

Hearing—I got to listen to Kati read a story she had written for school. It was awesome—great job KatiLouLou!!

Hair—I still have mine and today I was able to have it cut and colored. Thanks Gwen!

Hugs —Emma, who will turn 4 tomorrow sat on my lap and gave me tons of hugs this afternoon. Happy B-Day Emma.

Attitude is everything!!

Hugs, Teri

Sunday, December 13, 2009

. . . I had a great weekend. Not too busy—seems like the weekdays are more busy than the weekends. I am just saying "yes" to every-

thing, don't want to miss out. Fanny is resting
up for Tuesday, she might attend a party/lunch
or two mid-week.

Thought this was a cute saying: When
you get to the end of your rope, tie a knot, hang
on, and swing!!

I felt a new incentive to encourage others to embrace life and
health. I started peppering my blog with the questions like,
"What is your goal?" I challenged people to sign up for races
with me. I was inspired and motivated by my troops. In leading
the charge, I felt like I was tackling cancer head-on.

Monday November 2, 2009

I have had a great couple of days. Went on a
long ride, 3+ hours, with PJ on Sunday. Had
a good time running about 7 miles today and
going swimming with the swim girls tomorrow.
I am staying motivated because I signed up
to do the Ironman 70.3 Branson in September
2010. This is a half Ironman distance race and
I [am] hoping to be well enough to compete by
then. So, this is my goal. What's yours?

Thursday, November 5, 2009

I have had many emails, phone calls, and

personal conversations over this "what is your goal" deal. I love it. I had lunch today with my dear friends from high school—Lisa and Liz (AKA Elizabeth)—by the end of the lunch they agreed to train for the GO! St. Louis Half Marathon. They are going to kill me for putting this in my blog . . .

Surgery was scheduled for January 18, 2010. The doctors decided to attempt a surgical doubleheader: the colorectal surgeon would perform the colon resection and then pass the baton to the liver surgeon, who would then remove both tumors on my liver.

O.K.—Phase three of the ground war—surgery!!! I [cannot] believe it is finally here. I am relioved and at the same time scared. To think we started this battle 4 months ago. What a thought.

The surgery should begin around 8:30 and last 6 to 8 hours. The longer the surgery takes the better—meaning my doctors can remove more of the cancer.

I know the army is ready . . . armed with prayers . . .

Dave and I arrived at the hospital by 6:00 a.m. and immediately pre-op began. Dave stayed by my side the entire time, until

I was finally wheeled into surgery. The surgery took over eight hours. It was a tortuous wait for Dave. He received occasional updates from Julie, who was able to track my progress through the procedure. Sitting in the hospital cafeteria, he relayed Julie's updates via text and email to our family and friends.

The colon surgeon went first, removing the tumor near my cecum. Then the liver surgeon stepped in, slicing out the two tumors that had grown on either side of my liver. The surgery went smoothly. My biggest fear was that I would need a colostomy bag. The tumor was so low the surgeon couldn't guarantee I wouldn't need one. He would know for sure only once he cut me open and saw the exact size and location of the tumor.

The anesthesia was still going strong by the time Dave walked up to my bed in the recovery room. I was completely out of it. But in the midst of my drugged-induced sleep, I managed to open my eyes for a fraction of a second.

"Do I have a colostomy bag?" I asked, as if I hadn't been unconscious for the past nine hours.

"No. You don't have a colostomy bag."

"Thank God . . ."

And then I immediately fell back asleep.

Later that day, Mimi reported back to the army for me:

It is said that you must be scared before you can be courageous. Well, Teri was scared and rightly so . . . but oh my how courageous!

Thank you for your prayers and support today because THEY WORKED.

Teri's doctors were pleased with the results and all went as expected.

Teri sends her love,
Mimi

I eventually resumed updating my journal about my recovery. I wasn't recovering as quickly as we had expected. I tried to stay positive, but it soon became apparent that something was very wrong.

Friday, January 22, 2010

Day Four Post-Op . . . I thought I would be feeling better.

Doctors say I am doing great, but it has been more of a challenge than I anticipated. I feel like all I do is walk and sleep. Well, that is all I do!

My new "marathons" are walking around the halls. Yesterday I went four loops around five different times. Just need to refocus and set different kinds of goals. Kinda like life, I guess.

I am really anxious to get home, but I will need to "exercise" my patience....

Saturday, January 23, 2010

DAY 5 . . . Things are going well, just a little trouble controlling the pain. Today is better than yesterday and I am sure tomorrow will be better than today.

I can eat real food now and pretty much can eat whatever I feel I can tolerate. Yum, yum . . .

Wednesday, January 27, 1010

Since Friday I have had pain management issues due to a small surgical complication. I have not felt well and have not been in the mood to communicate. I have received many blessings this week, but am asking for some extra prayers for the surgical site to heal and for the pain to be controlled . . .

Thursday, February 4, 2010

Every day is a new day. Some days I feel better [than] others, but I am making progress, just slower than I ever thought. I am grateful for the successful surgery and most eager to get back "on track . . ."

Three weeks after my surgery, the pain was unbearable, even with medication. I had been sent home from the hospital, but the pain wasn't subsiding. Instead, it was escalating. It hurt to move. It hurt to breathe. It hurt to sleep. Nothing I did eased the pain. No amount of rest or medicine helped. With every passing day, my condition worsened. The pain overwhelmed my body and became my entire existence. I was thrown into a deep depression.

Kati remembers seeing me cry all day and all night. I never cried and never complained about pain. She would ask me why I was crying. "It just hurts really bad," I'd say and then keep crying. It was awful. Devastatingly awful.

Something wasn't right. I was no stranger to suffering. For the past three years I had done nothing but train to withstand pain and extreme discomfort. Yes, I knew recovery would be hard, but this was insupportable. Several times I called the hospital. Post-op pain was normal, they assured me before doubling my pain medication. It didn't help.

Late one night, Kati decided enough was enough. She called Liz and Lisa, my friends from high school.

"I don't know what to do," she cried into the phone when Liz answered. "I need help. My mom really needs you guys. She really needs you guys to come over. My mom is crying and really upset."

Liz called Lisa. "Kati called. She wants us to come over in the morning."

Lisa hesitated. She knew that if I were feeling as bad as Kati said, I wouldn't want visitors. I was never one for sympathy.

"No . . . I'm not going to just barge in."

But Liz would. She and her daughter Sallie, who was Kati's age, showed up at our door early the next morning. They came bearing gifts: a cargo load of bagels and Liz's high school yearbooks from Viz. It wasn't the first time Liz had surprised me with an unannounced delivery. In high school, we would celebrate classmates' birthdays by giving little gifts and knick-knacks. Because my birthday is in July, my birthday was never celebrated in school. So, on my sixteenth birthday, Liz hopped in her family's Oldsmobile Cutlass Supreme and drove to our house, where she proudly presented me with a gift: Watermelon Lip Smacker lip gloss. Three decades later, Liz knew looking at old pictures and sharing stories of our teenage shenanigans would cheer me up.

But she wasn't prepared for how bad I looked. I was crumpled on the couch, my body shaking with sobs. After a few minutes of greetings and hugs, Liz called Lisa.

"Get over here now," she demanded through the phone. "Teri needs us."

Lisa jumped in her car the minute she hung up the phone.

The company was needed. Surrounded by Liz, Lisa, Kati, and Sallie, I called Whitfield and sobbed into the phone that Kati would not be attending classes that day. Then I called Sallie's high school and left the same sobbing message. I wanted to let the teachers know that I needed the girls with me that morning. The last call was to Lisa's daughter Ali, who was at Butler University. We put her on speakerphone.

Before cancer, I never made myself vulnerable to anyone. I never got upset in front of people. I wasn't overly affectionate. I wasn't a hugger. I would have died before I cried in front of anyone. I was perpetually guarded. But I couldn't stay closed up anymore. I was broken.

That day, as the six of us talked and cried and laughed and cried some more, the walls began to come down. I felt safe with Liz and Lisa. There are some friends with whom you feel especially safe, friends you know will be there through thick and thin, when you need them most. Liz and Lisa and their daughters were those friends. And I was finally open to receive support and comfort. It was so freeing.

But while my spirit was lifted that morning, the pain still ravaged my body. Even the girls knew there was something physically wrong. I made another trip to Barnes, this time for a CT scan of my abdomen. Nothing unusual showed up, and I was sent home. The pain and depression continued.

The crisis came to a head just over a week later. My mom was at our house, watching the Olympics with me, when I suddenly burst into tears. I couldn't stop crying. My mom was beside herself, angry that I was still suffering so severely. She marched downstairs to find Dave. Dave immediately called the hospital. It was Sunday; I already had an appointment on Tuesday. The nurse said that as long as nothing changed for the worse, I should just come in as scheduled.

Despite the severity of the pain, we waited. I was unspeakably and irrationally emotional I physically could not stop crying but we didn't know what was going on. I had just had surgery. I had two very large incisions in my body. I was still coming off heavy anesthesia. The reality of my cancer diagnosis was still very raw. Certainly the pain and crying could be explained by any one of these factors; how much more all of them combined? We thought perhaps it was simply a perfect storm.

Dr. Tan's nurse practitioner, Beth, called on Monday morning to see how I was doing. I told her I was really sick, but that I had an appointment the next day.

Dave took me to the hospital in the morning. The minute Dr. Tan and Beth saw me, they knew it was bad. I looked awful. And there was a growing pink circle on my abdomen. An infection had been festering at the site of the surgical drain. I was septic. Dr. Tan immediately moved me to the treatment room. I was pumped with fluids and antibiotics. I spent the next seven days in the hospital, receiving antibiotics the whole time. The situation was serious, and the doctors and nurses monitored me closely until the infection was gone. Finally, I was sent home.

I returned a few weeks later to begin the process of removing the drain. The liver surgeon, Dr. Chapman, wanted to pull the tube out only a few inches, wait twenty-four hours, and then remove the drain completely. This way he could make sure the surgical site was fully healed and wouldn't collect fluid. If the site was clear after the trial period, he would remove the rest of the drain.

With the drain partially pulled, I left the hospital. An hour later, I was struck with an intense, stabbing sensation in my shoulder. The pain lasted the rest of the evening. When I returned the next day, I endured yet another CT scan. The tube had floated up and was pressing against my diaphragm. The pain in my shoulder had been an instance of "referred pain," or pain felt in an area other than the actual source, which in my case was my abdomen. But the CT scan also revealed that no fluid had accumulated at the surgical site. Dr. Chapman removed the drain, the shoulder pain evaporated, I was sent home, and—finally—for the first time, my body was given a fair chance to recover.

Sunday, February 28, 2010

Not sure how to open this entry.

It has been tougher than I ever imagined. I came home from the hospital late Tuesday but was still pretty fragile. Last Friday was the first day since surgery that I actually felt a glimmer of the old me. Praying for only forward progress now.

This past week was an awakening. I finally went through the "why me?" phase. Along with anger, doubt, exhaustion, frustration, and fear [has] come some healing—physically and emotionally. I am sure I will cycle through this again but next time I will be better prepared.

I feel like I have let the troops down. I missed the communicating and the relief from writing. I know you all have continued to pray for me and march on even when I have been out of touch. Just want each and every [one] of you to know how important you are to me. I have been given a new level of appreciation . . .

11

THE RETURN

C hemo resumed on March 16, the first of seven more rounds. I finally had the fiendish surgical drain removed from my abdomen the week before. I received a CT scan before the removal attempt to make sure there was no fluid or any other hindrance that would inhibit success. But the scan was clear, the hooligan tube was pulled out, and I was finally free of my "grenade."

I was not, however, free of Fanny. Round six of chemo—the first after reengaging post-surgery—meant the return of chemo homework. "I will come home with Fanny (guess I will need to dust her off)," I wrote in my journal. "So, we will bond for another 48 hours." Several days later I added, "I know Fanny was happy to see me. We bonded and now she is resting."

But if I was healthy enough for heavy chemo, I was healthy enough to train. At least, that was my logic. Liberated from the drain and recovered from the infection, I dove into training once more, quite literally when I rejoined my master's group at the pool. Chemo and training marched hand in hand through my journal. "Started round six and came home with Fanny," I wrote in one entry. "Feeling pretty good—biggest complaint—sore from yesterday's run . . ."

Dave continued to be my unwavering companion and a pillar of strength. Every Tuesday, he'd leave the office to meet me at Siteman for my chemo treatment. Mimi was my chauffer and comrade-in-arms. Dave and Mimi were my mainstays of practicality and application, documenting my treatment like they were watching a baseball game, scorecard in hand. No hit, no throw, no force out went unnoticed. They asked questions. They took notes. 6-4-3.

Kati often showed up, skipping a class or two so she could sit with me. Her visits were frequent, and I worried Kati's teachers at Whitfield would begin to take exception to her absence.

"Kati, we have only so many cancer cards in the deck," I would say. "We can't use them up all at once!"

I tried to get her to spread her visits out a bit more, but her teachers never said anything, and she visited often.

Kyle called often to see how I was doing and, when he was in town from SMU, he'd come with me to treatment. Kyle's visits were a great highlight, and they gave me something to look forward to. We all missed him so much. JoAnn also sat with me during treatments when she'd make her way to St. Louis from Columbia. I'm pretty sure I drove the nurses crazy because I always had a circus of family members with me, but it was a wonderful blessing. I appreciated the kids' visits especially, but their presence stirred mixed feelings. The realities of the treatment room could be harsh. There, lined up in rows of ascetic recliners, were the many different stages of cancer, illustrated in human flesh. Yes, I was strong, but there were others whose tenuous bodies and aged, careworn faces betrayed the length and strain of their physical battles. I looked healthy. They did not. Theirs were quiet corners, where fatigued loved ones sat by their sides, silent in long suffering. I didn't want the kids to look around the room and think the grim images represented my own future.

In April, my body launched another counteroffensive, this time through an allergic reaction to the chemo. It is not uncommon to develop sensitivity to chemotherapy several rounds into treatment. A delayed onset reaction, if it occurs, usually happens sometime between the sixth and eighth rounds. My body responded right on schedule. Again, it was Mimi who said something.

I had just finished my sixth chemo treatment and was being outfitted with Fanny.

"Teri," Mimi said, "your face is a little red."

I was unconcerned. I had returned from Florida only a few days before; the redness, I figured, was from my time in the sun. We climbed in the car. Again, Mimi looked at me.

"Ter, really. Your face. You should look at it."

I flipped down the passenger seat visor and looked in the mirror.

"Oh, wow. This isn't right."

"Do you want to go back in?"

"No, I'm fine."

"Are you sure?"

"Yeah."

Five minutes later, we were back at the house. I headed upstairs. My throat felt thick. It was difficult to swallow. By the time I saw my reflection in the master bathroom mirror, giant cherry splotches covered my face and neck. I immediately headed back downstairs, and Mimi drove me back to the hospital. But again I changed my mind before we even walked through the doors.

"You know, I think I'm better," I said, "Let's go home." It wasn't exactly a lie. Swallowing was still a challenge, but it wasn't worse. Surely it would pass.

Mimi shook her head. "No. No way. I'm not taking you back home. I told you there was something wrong with you!" She was exasperated. "Why won't you listen to me?"

She dropped me off at the door and parked the car. The nurse took one look at me, plopped me into a wheelchair, and called Dr. Tan. I had indeed suffered an allergic reaction to the chemo. The good news was we could continue treatment. By administering the medicine slowly and gradually, we could temper my body's response. The bad news was that each chemo treatment would now take nine hours. Nine hours in the chair. Nine hours in the treatment room. Every other week. Mimi was there for the whole of every treatment. From that point on, she stared at me constantly, watching for any signs of further complication.

Tuesday, April 13, 2010

After blood work and meeting with the doctor came the 9-hour-plus infusion at the hospital. And, yes, Fanny came home all loaded for her 48 hours of work . . .

Needless to say, it was a loooong day. I did have two very fun visitors—Anne and Noreen—some swim friends. And, of course, they came loaded with treats and important reading materials (STAR, In Touch, and PEOPLE!) . . .

I have got to say I am feeling really great. I have gotten to do so many different things and had such good times with so many people. Also been training and building some strength. I hope you have too . . .

I returned to training in earnest in late spring. (My previous multi-hour bike rides and ten-mile runs had been "base fitness" exercises. The Ironman bar, once raised, does not easily concede.) I signed up for the New Town Triathlon, a middle distance race in July. It would be a good measuring stick for Branson. When I first picked the half Ironman, a race exactly one year after my diagnosis, I figured I would have more time to train. I didn't anticipate the complications caused by the infection. Nor did I foresee the delays caused by low white blood cell counts.

Chemotherapy kills fast-dividing cancer cells—that's its job—but it is a rather indiscriminate assassin. Vital white blood cells are often gunned down in the chemical crossfire.

Neutrophils are a type of white blood cell responsible for controlling bacterial infection. When white blood cell counts are low, a condition called leukopenia, the body is especially susceptible to infection and is unable to defend itself should one develop.

Several times throughout treatment, my neutrophils were too low, meaning my chemotherapy had to be delayed another week until the counts climbed back up. The hold-ups due to low white blood cell counts were devastating. One time, after my white blood cell count came back too low, I asked the nurses to run another test. I was convinced there had been a mistake. I had been feeling relatively strong. I had been gaining weight (a good thing). "Can you redo the test?" I asked. They just laughed.

Tuesday, May 25, 2010

. . . Still working on my swim, bike, run. Slowly my energy and endurance are improving. I am concerned that my goal of completing the half Ironman in Branson in mid-September might be just a dream. I guess I will see how the maintenance course goes—and keep dreaming. We all need something to look forward to—a goal. Don't we?

In June, another low white blood cell count and consequent delayed round of chemo was particularly devastating. I have to admit I cried a bit that time. I was so eager to get the big treatments over with. I asked the troops to pray for my white blood cell counts to multiply. I didn't want any more setbacks. I was impatient. I wanted to train. I wanted to move forward. Going to Siteman for treatment only to be sent home with another week of chemo added to the calendar was incredibly frustrating and upsetting. On those days, I had to focus on the positives—my family, my training, my army—to keep from being depressed.

But even when my blood cell counts were low, I could still swim and bike and run, and I barreled through my training schedule, dealing with the side effects of treatment as they came.

Training through chemo is like training with the flu. It's slow going. Overall fatigue was a constant hurdle, triggered by a wave of assailants, from the cancer itself to the chemotherapy to a simple lack of fuel. Nausea made it difficult to eat, much less consume enough calories for a triathlete in training. I started many workouts in caloric deficiency and with depleted energy levels, a state as physiologically practical as an empty gas tank at the start line of the Indy 500. Neuropathy was another symptom of treatment. The numbness in my fingers and toes made it difficult to shift gears on my bike. My feet often felt heavy and numb—like the feeling you get when your foot falls asleep. The numbness threw off my balance and made running uncomfortable and at times disorienting. I would also get terrible muscle cramps. My hands and feet cramped on a daily basis. When I swam, my legs and feet would seize so badly I'd have to stop until I could move again. And I developed an unbearable sensitivity to the cold. Air conditioning, chilly water, a cool breeze—anything. I was painfully cold all the time. It was torturous.

However, the most draining aspect both mentally and physically was the simple scarcity of time that my body felt "normal." Such is the cycle of chemo: bring the body to its lowest common denominator of cellular survival, let it recover, and then move in for another strike as soon as it is healthy enough to withstand the cytotoxic onslaught. Just when you start to feel normal—literally that day—you go back for another treatment.

Even so, I had to continue training.

Monday, June 7th, 201

. . . Still swimming, biking, and running. If I told you how much you would call me crazy. The oncology nurse the other day called me unusual, and I laughed. Then she said, I mean what you are able to do is extraordinary, and I smiled. I [cannot] begin to express how grateful I am for the ability to train and for those who let me train with them . . .

That summer, I was given a glimpse of the chemo finish line. It was somewhat of a duplicitous denouement. At the end of the month, I would receive my twelfth and final round of chemo. The nine-hour infusion days would finally be over, as would my romance with Fanny, who, with the conclusion of chemo homework, would no longer be needed. No tears were shed.

Yet, it wouldn't be a tidy severance. Instead of an amicable split, I got a messy divorce settlement, with Siteman asserting its visitation rights until further notice. I would be placed on maintenance chemo, a regimen consisting of an hour-long infusion of anti-angiogenic medicine every other week, and seven days of oral chemo, four pills a day, on the same every-other-week schedule. In addition, I would receive CT scans and MRIs of my chest and abdomen every three months in order to monitor the other organs most likely to be affected by metastatic colon cancer. Unlike the primary chemo treatment, my maintenance chemo plan didn't—and still does not—have a termination date. My CEA, or carcino-embryonic antigen, a tumor marker for colorectal cancer, was still abnormal, indicating potential for new tumors to grow. Continued chemotherapy and periodic scans would help keep things in check.

It wasn't quite what I had hoped for or expected. Still, the end of heavy chemo was reason to celebrate, and celebrate I would.

My last big chemo treatment was scheduled for June 22. I would have a bell-ringing ceremony, and all the troops were invited. As it turned out, my white blood cell count did indeed end up being too low, and I had to delay round twelve. I went ahead with the ceremony, however, and was able to receive my final treatment the next day. I sent out the official summons, including an invitation to a post-treatment party.

To follow—A party at the Grieges's Mess Hall, right around the corner from Barnes. JoAnn and I are hoping many of you will stop by the house (maybe on [your] way home from work) so we can personally thank you for your

> prayers and support. Sandwiches, snacks,
> and cake will be served. I must give full
> disclosure—the bell is little and hangs in a
> hallway—but its significance is HUGE. This
> will mark the end of The Army's very success-
> ful 1st mission and the start of the next . . .

I had asked Siteman's head administrator if I could invite "some people" to my bell ceremony. Permission was granted, and "some" evinced itself in the form of over one hundred soldiers, much to the delighted alarm of the staff. Family, friends, training partners (including PJ, who wore full fatigues), and acquaintances filed through the glass doors by the dozens, gathering around the hallway where I stood in front of the little silver bell hanging discreetly on a wall just off the main lobby. Yes, the bell was small, and the tinny clang it made was hardly much bigger, even as it echoed down the hall. But to me and my army, the sound was deafening. It was a valorous, swashbuckling declaration of victory.

* * *

In July I raced my first tri since my diagnosis nearly a year before, the New Town triathlon. The race was an odd distance, longer than a typical sprint tri but shorter than an Olympic distance. Cristel, my ever-faithful training companion, raced as well; Kati and a small gaggle of friends tagged along as my support crew.

I felt strong in the water, though it wasn't my best swim; somewhat surprisingly, I had a great bike. But it was the run that caused me to worry. My feet felt like they were in cement buckets. Each step felt more sluggish than the last. I consoled myself with the knowledge that I had received chemo only days before and was undoubtedly suffering the effects. I put the race behind me and focused on my upcoming half Ironman.

By the time the half Ironman rolled around, I was two months into a steady routine of bi-weekly maintenance chemo infusion and pills. The race would be a test of my recovered fitness and endurance . . . and then some. Nestled in the hills of the Ozark Mountains, Branson presents one of the more challenging half Ironman courses on the market. Namely, it is very hilly, which really shouldn't be surprising, considering the course is described as being nestled in the hills of a mountain range.

In Branson, the hills come during the bike. The elevation chart for the bike course reads like a hospital heart monitor, with the illustrative line stabbing its way across the screen with sharp and terrifying consistency. Because the course is a loop, competitors ride the same stretch of road several times. The repetition of long, steep climbs is demoralizing. But if the bike elevation chart tracks the heartbeat of a living man—and a robustly energetic one at that— the run course elevation is clearly of someone less fortunate. For competitors whose legs have been systematically destroyed by the ascents, the pancake-flat run is somewhat of a relief. That is, as long as they can get over the black asphalt and Indian summer heat that effectively makes the run as pleasant as a frying pan.

My army was there in the form of my immediate family, my nieces, and close friends. In an incredible show of support, Dave, JoAnn's daughter Cary, and Ruben did the half Ironman relay. Here I was competing for the first time since I found out I had cancer, and my husband, my niece, and my friend (who just happened to be the gastroenterologist who diagnosed me) were out on the course competing too. Knowing they were out there motivated me even more.

I had a good swim and was halfway through the bike before Jeff was able to catch up to me. (My wave had started way before his.) The turnaround for the bike is at the top of a mammoth climb, the kind of ascent that slows cadence speeds to a tromping lumber at best and a standstill at worst.

"What is that?" Jeff said as he pulled even with me on the hill. "Oh, I think I just saw some cancer fall out of your ass." He smiled. "How you feeling, girl?"

"I feel great!" I answered between breaths. "Really, I feel great!"

Jeff raised his hand to give me a fist bump. I tried to return the bump, but somehow I ended up crashing my bike to the ground. To this day Jeff claims I crashed because I was trying to hug him. To this day I swear I wasn't. I was just trying to return the fist bump. And in the process, I completely wiped out.

I was uninjured, but I was still on a giant hill. I climbed back on my bike and tried to pedal. The incline was too steep, and I nearly fell for a second time. I tried again. No luck. Finally—I'm still not quite sure how I managed it—I found myself back in the saddle and moving forward.

Other than the unfortunate bike crash and a lost timing chip that fell off somewhere in the transition from the swim to the bike, Branson was a rousing victory. The buckets that had cemented themselves to my feet in New Town never made an appearance, and I cruised the run without needing to walk or stop. I was back . . . almost. A full return, in my mind, required, well, a full.

Four weeks after Branson, I signed up for Ironman Florida.

The race was exactly a year out. Jeff and Scott signed up as well. Jeff also returned to his position as my coach. He wrote a highly personalized program designed with both my perennial training habits and chemo treatments in mind. Jeff has always been very aware of how important it is to keep going and to set goals. His mentality is that if you're gonna die, you may as well go out doing what you love.

But there was more to my plan than just another Ironman. Yes, I was signed up for Florida. Yes, I would train for Florida. But Florida would be my default race. I wanted to do Kona.

Fittingly, the idea had struck me in Hawaii, when Dave and I had traveled to the Big Island to watch Scott race. I can still remember sitting on Ali'i Drive, the famous main artery along the Kona coast that leads athletes to and from the finish line of the Ironman World Championship, watching the pro athletes sprint the final miles of the race. The memory is so vivid. It was October 2009, two weeks after my diagnosis.

Soon after signing up for Ironman Florida, I began my quest for a spot on the Big Island. I started a wholesale inquisition of anybody and everybody even remotely involved in the triathlon world, asking for information about sponsors, about contacts, about applying as a special interest story. Several of my family and friends started championing my cause as well, writing letters and sending emails to Ironman. But months passed, and still I didn't hear a response. Finally, in June, I fired a haphazard email to Peter Henning, a producer at NBC

Ironman Productions. I told him my story. I told him I had a bucket list: to see Kati and Kyle get married, to celebrate my twenty-fifth wedding anniversary, and to race the Ironman World Championship. I told him that perhaps, like Jon Blais had been before me, I could be a human interest story.

> Dear Mr. Henning,
> My name is Teri Griege and I am an Ironman. I ask that you please read my letter before you hit delete. In August of 2008 I completed Ironman Louisville (my first Ironman at age 47) and came 5 minutes and one slot short of qualifying for Kona. Determined to qualify the next year, I trained and trained. Two weeks after completing Ironman Louisville 2009 I was [diagnosed] with stage 4 colon cancer with metastasis to my liver. Of course, I did not qualify, but [I] had a very respectful time of under 12:30.
> I am writing to you hoping to gain consideration as a special interest story. I decided I wanted to be an Ironman after watching the 2005 World Championship program featuring Jon Blais. Tears rolled down my cheeks at the conclusion of the program. I believe my story should be told: 1) to save lives and 2) to inspire. No one could believe that I had just completed an Ironman and 14 days later found to be full of cancer—not the doctors, not me, not my family or friends. I was the picture of health. I

completed radiation and had 5 rounds of heavy chemotherapy to shrink the tumors, hoping to make them operable. By January 2010 I was ready for surgery. I had a colon resection—removing 12 inches of colon—and a liver resection removing almost 70% of my liver. I had a very difficult post-op recovery due to infections. I then completed 8 more rounds of heavy chemotherapy. In August 2010 I was placed on maintenance chemotherapy, which I am still receiving and probably always will. The regime consists of one week on, one week off. My goal last summer was to race 70.3 Branson, which I did. This year I will race 70.3 Kansas and Ironman Florida.

I really cannot convey to you in an email my story, my dreams, my heart. I just ask that you please take the time to speak with me. I realize the 5-year survival rate for stage 4 colon cancer is low—some say 6%. The constant chemotherapy is taking a toll on me and I now realize that endurance sports will not be a part of my life much longer. Physically this will be the last year I think I will be able to complete a full Ironman. Top 3 on my bucket list: 1) see my children get married, 2) celebrate 25 years of marriage, 3) participate in the 2011 Ironman World Championship. I turn 50 on July 17th. Please consider making my dream come true.

Sincerely,
Teri Griege

Peter responded the next day. I was shocked. I really hadn't expected to hear anything in response to my email. To that point, all of our efforts had been unavailing. But now NBC was interested in my story.

Peter said he was out of the country for an Ironman and told me to call him when he was back in the United States. I did. I told him my story in detail. He said he'd have an answer for me in a couple of weeks. I was encouraged by our conversation and the attention from NBC, but I knew that nothing was guaranteed. Every year, NBC and Ironman are inundated with similar requests from people who have incredibly worthy and inspiring stories. The chances of being selected are slim.

On Tuesday, July 5, just three months before the Ironman World Championship, Mimi, JoAnn, and I sat in the waiting room at Siteman. I always turned off the sound on my phone when I went in for treatment, but occasionally I'd check the screen. One missed call. There was a voicemail.

It was NBC. I was in.

12

BIG ISLAND CALLING

A slot in the Ironman World Championship is a double-edged sword. Yes, it will gain you admittance to the biggest rock concert in triathlon. But it's a pricey ticket, one that tempers elation and engenders panic. It hits you the moment you step out the door for a run and realize that none of your previous training has prepared you for what you will face in Hawaii. No other race can duplicate the conditions of an island race that marries volcanic, equatorial, mountainous, tropical, and desert conditions in vengeful polygamy. In Kona, precision must be reconciled with chaos, and nothing you do beforehand can fully prepare you for the collision.

Over the winter, I had maintained a solid base fitness. I raced the GO! St. Louis Half Marathon in April and the Ironman Kansas 70.3 in June before entering what would be the summer of Kona. Cancer and chemo added new challenges to training, with the side effects of both disease and treatment invading my workouts. Nausea and lack of appetite made it difficult to eat enough to fuel my body. Maintaining a healthy bodyweight was a constant struggle. The neuropathy also persisted, though it wasn't severe. Fatigue was almost constant. I'd hop on the treadmill, run three miles, jump off, change the laundry, eat a banana, and then hop back on the treadmill for another three miles. I learned to listen to my body and what it needed. If I needed to catch my breath, I'd rest. If I needed fuel, I'd eat. I had to keep my approach to training simple. Get in the miles and let the rest work itself out.

I reinstated hills into my training program to prepare for the mountains of Kona. At least once a week I'd make the trek to Babler Park in Wildwood where hills are the modus operandi. I also began running around the park behind my house, which was puckered with small hills like a rug caught in a door. The heat was old hat; I liked running during the hottest part of the day anyway. I still made my bi-weekly visits to Siteman for chemo. Treatment was a momentary pause in training. I'd get in tough workouts beforehand. Sometimes I'd run home straight from Siteman.

Pedal the Cause was another passion that provided me with a goal and a purpose. Pedal the Cause is an annual charity bike ride to raise money for cancer research, grants, and care at Siteman Cancer Center and St. Louis Children's Hospital. My team of cyclists was riding for a spunky, tenacious nine-year-old girl named Kaitlyn. Kaitlyn is a gymnast (her favorite thing to do is a "tuck," a backwards flip using no hands) and a straight-A student. Kaitlyn was eight years old when she won a gold medal in tumbling at the Junior Olympics. Two months later, she was diagnosed with stage III lymphoma. Once more, I established a clear goal: I wanted to be the top individual fundraiser. The year before, I raised over $30,000. This time around I had passed the $70,000 mark by late summer. I and my closest cycling friends—Cristel, PJ, and Diane—handed out T-shirts, conscripted cyclists and non-cyclists alike, hosted fundraising parties, and evangelized the cause. Kaitlyn, her short brown hair still inching its way back from chemo treatment, was by my side at every event. Kaitlyn and I became close friends— despite the forty-year age difference. We were cancer fighters, and our shared battle with the disease created a special bond. I tried to make as many of Kaitlyn's treatments and procedures as I could. She was my little sister-soldier in combat.

Meanwhile, in early June, JoAnn finished chemotherapy. It was a merciful end. JoAnn and her chemo treatments had clashed in a bitter eight-month conflict; the nature and severity of her symptoms were very unusual for the treatment she was receiving. Less than 2 percent of colon cancer patients lose their hair; JoAnn began losing hers after her first treatment. Her white blood cell counts also plummeted, and she had to receive a booster, Neupogen, before she could continue treatment. The delays in treatment—the days when she would show up for chemotherapy only to be told that the whole process would be delayed another week—were devastating. To make matters worse, the booster made her nauseated and fatigued, like she had the flu.

But the nausea from the Neupogen was penny-ante gambling compared to the side effects she suffered from the chemo itself. After the first treatment, she was severely nause-ated. By the second treatment, the nausea was constant and accompanied by a pungent, bitter flavor in her mouth—like dirt and metal—that made everything she ate taste rancid. Things went downhill from there. For over five months, JoAnn had no relief. Her nausea became so severe she needed pre-medication before each chemo treatment just so she could make it to treatment. The anti-nausea medicines did nothing. She couldn't eat. She couldn't sleep. She couldn't think. She had always been lean; she became gaunt and bony. Her face was cadaverous beneath a head with no hair. Her thick blonde tresses, usually styled to perfection, were gone. Friends didn't recognize her. Strangers thought she was dying. By the end of her treatment, she was so sick she begged her doctor to cut back on her chemo dosage.

But while outward appearances evidenced an altered and battered body, on the inside, JoAnn was still JoAnn, and she took whatever steps she could to substantiate her stalwart personality. Even at her sickest, she never left the house with-out makeup or earrings. Every chemo session. Every aerobics class. When the neuropathy in her hands became so severe she could no longer put her earrings in, she bought new earrings that were easier to fasten. She had no hair. She had no color in her face. But by golly, she had her earrings. She was still JoAnn.

Incredibly, JoAnn continued to teach aerobic class-es three days a week, though she was too weak to do the exercises herself. Instead, she'd sit on an exercise ball at the front of the room and talk the class through the motions while her daughter Cary demonstrated. Cary was JoAnn's Mimi; she went with her to every chemo treatment and aerobics class, driving her to and from her appointments and, with the help of Chuck, making sure her obstinate mom followed doctor's orders.

JoAnn also had a chemo homework kit in the form of a port implanted beneath her shoulder, a black fanny pack, and a clear, thin tube connecting the two. JoAnn called her port "The Alien" from the moment it was implanted. She resented her cancer diagnosis, and she disdained her port with equal passion. JoAnn's relationship with her treatment wasn't quite as amicable as mine was. I saw chemo as my lifeline: it was making me better and keeping me alive. JoAnn saw it as the enemy. I called chemo medicine. JoAnn called it poison. The port represented the mothership of evil. She refused to look at it. She refused to touch it. Thus, I had Fanny, and JoAnn had The Alien.

In June, JoAnn was emancipated from the bitter relationship. It was over a month before JoAnn finally began to feel normal. She had defeated her cancer. She had survived. Now it was time to help me do the same.

I remember very clearly my last chemo treatment before Kona. As always, Mimi was with me.

"Teri!"

A woman dressed in bright orange scrubs, a gray-and-orange "Pedal the Cause" T-shirt, and a matching gray warm-up jacket waltzed into the waiting room. Rosa, one of the nurses at Siteman, worked with me often.

"Here's my girl!" I exclaimed as Rosa struck a pose, right hand up, left hand on her hip, her large silver hoop earrings bouncing as she shook her head with dramatic vogue.

Mimi and I followed Rosa to a small alcove where a scale awaited me.

"I put on weight," I said.

Rosa tilted her head skeptically as she tested the truth of my statement. I had put on a pound. Maybe.

"Good for you," Rosa conceded. Gaining a pound wasn't much, but it was better than the alternative. "We've been watching you. You've been looking skinny."

"It's the Pop•Tart diet," I explained. "Pop•Tarts make me put on weight."

After a parade into yet another room, I hopped onto an exam table while Rosa performed the traditional liturgies, checking my blood pressure, temperature, and heart rate. The examination felt superfluous. I didn't look sick. I didn't feel sick. I was fit and ready to go.

"There's my main man," I said as Dr. Tan walked by. I turned to Rosa and lowered my voice, momentarily stopping the check-up. "He's coming to Kona."

Rosa's eyes widened in surprise.

"It is really cool."

"That *is* really cool," Rosa echoed.

A changing of the guards, and Rosa left as Beth, Dr. Tan's nurse practitioner, walked into the room, clipboard in hand. Beth reviewed the rearrangement of my treatment plan over the next two weeks. Because of the race, I would skip my next chemo treatment. I was two weeks out from Kona: I would get chemo this week, use the following week to recover, and then—if all went well—feel relatively normal just in time for race day the week after that.

"So, your next chemo will be post-Kona," Beth confirmed.

"We get home—" I paused—"that Wednesday? I can come by on the way home from the airport."

"Okay. Wednesday then."

Beth began another round of examination, checking my nutrient and mineral intake as well as my electrolyte levels. Skipping a chemo treatment isn't ideal—fighting a metastatic disease is a war of attrition, and the longer the battle, the greater the toll on the body—but a missed treatment isn't elective sabotage. Beth's primary concern was dehydration; namely, preventing it.

Every process in our bodies is driven by the potassium and sodium stored in our cells. When cells are depleted of these two essential minerals, they cease functioning correctly, and the negative repercussions permeate every bodily system, from digestive to musculoskeletal to neurological. Dehydration would directly impact the organs critical to the effectiveness of my chemo treatments, such as the kidney and liver, which filter both nutrients and medicines. It would also impede my body's ability to recover from workouts. Toxins are released from the lymphatic system during exercise; the liver, kidney, and spleen act as an effective waste management system, flushing the accumulated toxins from the body. When organ functions are compromised, the metabolic toxins build up, inhibiting muscle performance and causing tight ness, cramps, and spasms. The body's ability to break down protein and absorb essential amino acids is also inhibited, starving already fatigued muscles. Dehydration posed an especial danger, not only by nature of its specific effects, but because the intensity of Ironman training was perpetually draining my electrolyte stores.

Beth closely monitored my kidney and liver functions— how they were filtering and whether or not they were receiving enough fluid. She ran a metabolic panel to track vital electrolytes. If I was showing signs of dehydration or if my organs weren't filtering properly, chemo would have to be delayed yet again. Such symptoms would also pose an ill-favored omen; if I were dehydrated going into the race, there was very little chance I would cross the finish line. Or even come close.

"Should she come in before the race and get blood work done? Make sure everything is okay and she's ready to go?" Mimi asked.

She had been quiet from her perch in the corner of the room. Mimi was my reality check, a one-woman "Truth Squad," as Beth called her. When I didn't see something as an issue (or neglected to bring it up, which was usually the case), Mimi asked questions and gave details.

Beth agreed it would be a good idea to give me a liter of fluids right before the race.

"I gained weight," I reminded her, changing the subject.

"Oh, yeah? Good. We thought you looked thin coming in here."

"I put rocks in my pockets."

Beth smiled.

"It's the Pop•Tarts diet. Makes me gain weight."

Beth stood up from the desk where she had been making notes. "Let's do the routine."

"Oh, yeah . . . I forgot."

The check-up ceremonies continued. Beth listened to my heart.

"It's still beating," I assured her.

"Barely. It's so exercised."

After a few minutes, the procession moved on, this time to the treatment room for chemo infusion. I ignored my chair for another ten minutes. I had catching up to do with the nurses and patients and their support crews.

It hadn't been my intention, nor would I have ever expected the result, but people were paying attention to my training—and they in turn were taking action. That's not to say I didn't voice a few pointed inquiries at every visit. I'd flat out ask the nurses if they were exercising or what they were doing to work out. Many of them began running, walking, or biking—most for the first time in their lives. They bought elliptical machines. They were eating healthier. Dr. Tan hired a personal trainer. Beth, who had never been one to exercise, embarked on a daily walking regimen. A ninety-minute commute from her home in southern Illinois to Siteman in west St. Louis County made finding time for anything other than work—much less a workout—difficult. Still, each visit, I grilled her about her exercise routine. Soon she was walk ing seven to eight miles every day. Beth told me the staff's collective motivation was, "Well, if Teri can do it while going through chemo, we can do it."

I tried not to complain about chemo or my life being hijacked by an insidious disease, about the daily disruptions of treatment, or the constant fatigue and discomfort. I didn't deny them; I just never brought them up. Why should I? Everyone has his or her own cancer. Everyone has struggles and obstacles. Everyone has valid reasons to throw in the towel. Why would my situation justify excuses? It didn't. So I simply tried to keep doing what I loved. Action erases excuses. Action holds people accountable. Action keeps things real.

Eventually, I sat down for my thirty-minute IV infusion, though this time around it felt more like social hour as people stopped by my chair to chat. They knew I was doing Kona and that this was my last time at Siteman before the race.

"Did you hear?" I asked as Lisa, Siteman's head administrator, stopped by. "Dr. Tan is gonna come."

"Shut up!" Lisa responded.

"Shut up!" I said.

Just before treatment was done, Dr. Tan walked by and stopped at my chair.

"I'm so excited you're coming," I whispered.

"I'm excited, too," Dr. Tan replied in the same quiet voice.

The last of the medication dripped into my bloodstream. I took a slow breath as the nurse unhooked me from the IV machine. That was that. Next week, I'd be in Hawaii. Next week, I'd be free. Next week, I'd try to remember what life felt like before cancer.

13

KONA

The year was 1982. Julie Moss was a twenty three-year-old undergrad student and a surfer. She was also a physical education major without a senior thesis. Months away from graduation, she happened upon the last half of ABC's *Wide World of Sports*, which was airing a little known endurance triathlon event from Hawaii. Julie was mesmerized; the introduction was epiphanic. The Ironman would be her senior project. She would compete in the race and write about her experience. Forget that she knew nothing about training. She was fascinated. She needed a thesis. It was a no-brainer.

As a proverbial stone-broke college student, Julie had to convince her mom to pay for the trip. Her only training manual was a single article she had read in *Sports Illustrated*. Even then, she didn't start training in earnest until December, after classes ended. Two months of training would be plenty, she figured.

On race morning, Julie waded into the waters of Kailua Bay, an unknown undergrad student whose only goal was to cross the finish line. But by mile eight in the marathon, Julie Moss found herself leading the race.

The ABC cameras circled around her. Who was this girl? The second-place woman, Kathleen McCartney, a stud triathlete who had come to Kona to win, wasn't even in sight. Mile ten. Mile fifteen. Mile twenty. Wearing a tractor cap she got for free in the race swag bag and a sports bra she finagled mid-race from a volunteer after her own broke, Julie held first place. By a lot.

But the day was beginning to take its toll on her body. Over ten hours had passed since the start of the race. Ten hours in the heat, in the sun, in the wind. By mile twenty-five, her lead over McCartney was still six minutes. She kept running.

The finish line was only a few hundred yards away when Julie's knees buckled for the first time. She collapsed on the asphalt. Propping her torso up with her arms, she tried to straighten out her legs. Her brain told her body to get up, but her muscles refused to fire. She pulled her knees under her and tried to stand, but once more her exhausted body crumpled to the pavement. Volunteers and spectators rushed to her side to help; in desperation she waved them away. Finally, she struggled her way to her feet and began running again. She ran, she stumbled, she walked, she stumbled, she ran some more. Her body was shutting down. Her determination was not. Two hundred yards from victory, Julie collapsed again. She knew McCartney was chasing her. Forcing herself to her hands and knees, she began crawling.

Fifteen feet from the finish line, Julie saw a blur of legs as they whooshed by, strong and light. The vision lasted only a moment, a glimpse of flesh from the corner of her eye, but it was enough. She knew.

McCartney was unaware of Julie's crisis when she passed her, the crowd around her fallen competitor being too large and confusing. Even when she crossed the finish line moments later, McCartney had to be told that she had won. Television cameras encircled her. Bulbs flashed. She was crowned the island's new champion.

Twenty-nine seconds later, Julie Moss crawled across the finish line in second place.

A spellbound nation watched as the drama on Ali'i Drive unfolded. The image of the young woman dragging her broken body down the final yards of an impossibly long and grueling contest catapulted the Ironman into the national spotlight as a stunned audience found themselves riveted by what they had just witnessed. Who was this girl and what was this race whose participants sacrificed body and spirit not for the chance to win, but merely the chance to finish?

Quite simply, this was Kona.

The Island of Hawai'i is a captivating seductress, simultaneously tantalizing and tranquil. Framed by cobalt waters, an undulating shoreline softens the sharp mountain peaks, a lush perimeter diluting a severe landscape emanating from a volcanic core. The island beguiled Captain James Cook, kissing his feet before sentencing him to an inglorious death on its amorous shores. It served as a regal throne for the warrior-king Kamehameha I, who united the Hawaiian archipelago into a royal kingdom after years of bloody conflict. In Hawaiian mythology, it is the land of refuge for the volatile deity Madame Pele, goddess of volcanoes, who was driven from her homeland after seducing her sister's husband and who is said to roam the streets disguised as an old woman. The island's tempestuous nature is attributed to Pele's battles with other goddesses over lovers (whom she has a habit of killing post-nuptials), and misfortune following an excursion to the island is ascribed to curses on artless visitors who pilfer a souvenir or two from her black shores.

The Big Island, as the Island of Hawai'i is better known, is the tumultuous offspring of five volcanoes, two of which—Mauna Loa and Kilauea—are still active. The island itself is only ninety-three miles across at its widest point; yet it is bigger than all the other Hawaiian islands combined. Crammed within its borders are eight to eleven of the world's thirteen climate zones (depending on whom you ask). Snow-covered mountain peaks slope to desolate lowlands, and verdant tropical rainforests bleed into arid deserts, the latter dominating the landscape of the Big Island. The Kona district, home of the Ironman World Championship, lies on the leeward—or dry—side of the island, where black fields stretch on for miles, gullied and scarred with the dried-up veins of lava flow. On this side of the island, the ground looks charred and forsaken—probably because it is, a topographical masterpiece of molten efflux hardened into black lava deserts. Yet this same austere and solemn landscape nurtures succulent papaya farms and opulent orchid gardens, so many, in fact, that the island is called "The Orchid Isle." Lava sizzles and hisses on beaches

just steps away from roadside stands heaped with meaty maca-
damia nuts and exotic harvests of mango, guava, cinnamon,
and allspice. On the Big Island, the spartan and the lavish exist
in fickle tension, for the Big Island, like its mistress Pele, is a
jealous and capricious lover. That is part of its allure. That is
part of its legend.

* * *

"Oh, no!" Cristel exclaimed as she maneuvered the rental car
down Ali'i Drive. "We missed the Underpants Run!"

The Underpants Run, held two days before the race, is
an annual exhibition in downtown Kona. As the name
suggests, the run is a pageant of speedos, tighty-whities, and
bikinis, many of which are colorfully—if not exactly tastefully—
decorated with national flags. A few festive athletes were still
milling along the road, the only remnants of the morning's
flamboyant run.

Arriving in Kona during the Ironman World Championship is like landing on another planet. Lean, tight bodies with chiseled abs and carved legs swarm the streets,
concentrated onto a tiny strip of Ali'i Drive. They glisten
with sweat as they log their final miles in the thick island humidity. They drip with saltwater, fresh from a swim in Kailua
Bay. They whoosh by on sleek, pristine bikes, aerodynamic
in form and motion. Demigod pedestrians saunter in the
sun, carrying backpacks and water bottles. It is a somatic
spectacle where clothes are a hindrance and no calorie is left
uncounted. It is enough to make even the extremely fit feel
like flabby transplants.

Once we arrived downtown, I changed into my swimsuit and descended the clumsy stone steps leading into Kailua Bay. My first swim had been two days before, when the swells had been so rough I climbed out of the water seasick—and to the admonition of JoAnn, who had come to the terrifying conclusion that I had drowned. (I had told JoAnn I would be back in twenty minutes. Instead, I met a couple of South Africans by the buoys and we embarked on a two-mile workout.)

My schedule was tight leading up to race day. Since NBC was featuring my story in the broadcast, I bounced from one event to another, all while trying to prepare for my own race. Between packet pick-up, athlete check-in, mandatory pre-race meetings, bike check-in, transition prep, and meet-and-greets, I squeezed in pre-race swims, bikes, and runs. Cristel and Ruben joined me on a reconnaissance ride to Hawi, the infamous turnaround point of the Ironman World Championship bike course. We battled severe crosswinds during the entire forty-mile ride, prompting a trip to a local bike shop for wheel surgery. The wheels I was using had caught too much wind on the way to Hawi; several times I was literally blown halfway across the road. Cristel's wheels were better suited to the conditions. She generously suggested (read: demanded) I use her wheels. I took her up on her offer, and we made the switch.

In addition to my immediate family—Dave, Kyle, Kati, Laverne, Mimi, and JoAnn—a sweeping contingent of the army made the transpacific journey to Kona: Mimi's daughters Christi and Courtney; JoAnn's daughters Julie and Cary, the latter bringing her oldest son Wilson (who, at twelve years of age, was my chivalrous protector); Dave's brothers

Mark and Chuck and their wives, Peggy and Jessica; Dave's
sister Kathy; my triathlon husbands, Jeff and Scott; Cristel and
Rubin; Dave's business partner John Frank and his wife Jan;
our friends Paul and Kathy Fullerton, Joseph Scherer, Tom
and Sue Cox, and Kathy Pietoso; Dr. Seiichi Noda, a St. Louis
triathlon fixture who would also be a medical volunteer at the
race; and, of course, Dr. Tan and his wife Elizabeth. It was a
fantastic deployment of troops, over thirty soldiers strong.

After my short swim in the holy waters of Kailua
Bay, I hopped into another rental car, this time with Jeff and
Scott, and received a rundown of race-day strategies. Jeff
filtered through the technicalities and application of race-day
logistics; Scott's contributions were anecdotal.

"Palani is a great spectator part of the course—
everybody will be cheering and calling your name. You'll be
going slow," Scott said, referring to a section of the marathon
course on Palani Drive where miles one, ten, and twenty-five
converge. "It's a huge climb at mile ten."

I shook my head. "I'm gonna walk it. I'm not gonna
burn myself up."

Jeff jumped in with preventative race-day tactics.

"Teri, you've gotta keep your fluid intake about equal
to what you're expending. With your current meds—" he
shook his head—"you need to get something that goes straight
to your stomach."

Jeff's biggest concern was keeping me fueled for a race
that could last as long as seventeen hours. Managing midrace
nutrition is its own science; and in Kona, it is an irregular
one. Triathletes can burn a staggering 8,000–10,000 calories
during an Ironman. In order to keep their bodies going, they
need to replace at least 30–50 percent of those calories while

they're racing—no simple assignment, and one that is tackled primarily on the bike, the longest leg of the race.

The bike is an exercise in multitasking, as athletes power their bikes along one hundred and twelve miles of steep hills, mind-numbing straightaways, and gale-force winds while slugging energy gel, snagging bananas from aid stations, and downing over a gallon of water, sports drinks, and flat Coke. Biking too hard or failing to consume enough calories and electrolytes is the most effective way to sabotage the run—and, effectively, the entire race. The bike is a make-or-break affair.

I jotted down Jeff's instructions—how much I should eat and drink and when—and placed the notes in a plastic wristband I'd wear during the race.

"So, what should my run be this afternoon? Forty-five minutes, tops?" I asked Jeff.

"Thirty tops. You've been on your feet way too much today." Jeff's expression was serious. He was always serious. "How tired are you right now?"

"Not very."

Jeff didn't buy it.

"I want you to go back, take an energy gel, take a giant drink, go for a thirty-minute run, and have someone cook you a monster meal while you run. Then you're gonna sit and eat for the next two hours, got it?"

"Got it."

"You've got a lot of catching up to do in your calorie intake. Got it?"

"Get it? Got it? Good."

Jeff shook his head. Occasionally, I can be a handful.

* * *

"Dave and I just want to thank all of you for coming," I said, addressing our family and friends scattered across a grassy lawn furnished with tiki torches and elegant tables draped in white linen. On Friday night, twelve hours before the race, my army gathered for an intimate outdoor meal overlooking the Pacific Ocean. Over thirty soldiers had reported for duty, and Dave and I wanted to treat them to dinner—a traditional pre-race pasta dinner, of course. I kept my address short, but I wanted to let everyone know how much it meant to me to have them there. I told the story of Jon Blais and described my dream of competing in the Ironman World Championship. I thanked everyone for coming, for their support, for their encouragement, for their love. I told them how supremely grateful I was for the opportunity to race, and how grateful I was to have such an incredible army.

"And did everyone get a T-shirt?" I ended my speech by dashing to a cardboard box filled with blue, jersey-style "Team Teri" T-shirts and visors.

The next hour was a frenzy of carbohydrates and conversation, as the troops posed for pictures, piled plates with pasta, and dug through the T-shirt box in an impromptu size exchange. The party was merry but short; the race demanded an early curfew for both athlete and spectators alike. One by one, the army filtered down the grassy path leading away from the festive lights glittering on the tiny lawn. One by one, I hugged my soldiers. I thanked them again and told them I would see them at the finish line.

Later that night, I crawled into bed. Dave was already asleep. For the first time that day, my stomach was calm—

though relief hadn't come without a price. I had thrown up several times while I was getting ready for bed. I chalked it up to nerves, excitement, maybe something I'd eaten. But whatever it had been was out of my stomach now. The nausea was gone. So were my nerves—for the most part anyway. I felt excited. I felt grateful. I felt happy. I was living the dream.

I hope I get some sleep . . .

It was my last thought before I did.

4:00 a.m. I pulled off the covers and swung my legs over the bed. I had laid my clothes out the night before; now I squinted as I pulled them on, only half able to see. Dave was up and had turned on the lights. I wasn't hungry, but I forced myself to eat a banana and half a bagel before Jeff and Scott arrived to chauffer me to the race start. They arrived within a few minutes. I kissed Dave and climbed into the car. It was a short and quiet ride. Maybe five minutes. Scott parked the car while Jeff and I made our way to the athlete's area. Finding my bike among the dimly lit rows, I made a few final additions—a couple of water bottles and some more GU—before heading to T2 to drop off the clothes I'd wear during the marathon. With my transitions ready and nothing left to do but wait, I made my way through the labyrinth of partitions and tents to find my family for a few final hugs.

There is a certain solemnity in the darkness before an Ironman. Athletes and their loved ones crowd beneath the glow of the finish line, hugging and wishing each other well. Yes, there is excitement, but in many ways it is subdued. The athletes know what awaits them. They know they will not return to this spot until many hours have passed. They know they will suffer. What they don't know—what no athlete ever knows—is how much.

I sat in the athlete's area and waited. At 6:30 a.m., the pro race began to the explosion of the starter's cannon. Even as the loud *boom!* resonated across the water and bounced off the stone walls encasing Kailua Pier, the age groupers began making their way to the sandy beach. Their race would begin in thirty minutes. Those who wanted a top position in the water swam out to the start line, approximately sixty yards from shore. Mass start swims in Ironman races are veritable slugfests as athletes battle for space, even climbing over the backs of other swimmers to get ahead. Those who want to start at the front of the pack can do so—as long as they're willing to tread water for twenty minutes before the race even begins. (Being at the front does not come without a price.)

My mission was to survive the swim without getting kicked in the face or being pushed underwater. I waited back by the bikes until most of the other athletes had made their way into the water. Finally, I waded into the bay. As I treaded water, waiting for the race to start, I spun around to look at the thousands of spectators sitting five people deep on the floodwall. Somehow I spotted Dave, Kyle, and Kati. They were waving. They were cheering me on. It was then, for the first time, that it hit me. This—all of this—was real. This was Kona. I was here. I was in the ocean waiting for the start of the Ironman World Championship.

I smiled and waved back at my family before turning to face a golden horizon suspended above the sapphire blue water. It was a fitting way to start the race of my life.

* * *

The desolation is what strikes you first. The loneliness. It impales you. Reaching as far as the eye can see—and then further still—is a harsh, monochromatic landscape buffeted by warmongering winds and a searing sun. This is not the Hawaii you see in perky travel brochures. Lush is nowhere to be found. This is a land inhospitable, the exposed peaks of a mammoth undersea mountain range formed by volcanic eruptions. The lava desert transfixes the eyes with an endless expanse of black rock and pontifical ascents and leaves you wondering how life can survive in such a barren landscape. It is bleak. It is lonely. It is the road to Hawi.

I leaned forward on my white Cannondale, elbows bent at right angles, back straight, head primed over the handlebars. The aero position is fast, but it's unstable, especially in the gusty temperament of the Queen Ka'ahumanu Highway—the "Queen K," as it is known. I held the position as long as I could.

Hawi (pronounced ha-VEE) is an unassuming town, nestled in relative obscurity except for its designation as the turnaround point of the bike course in the Ironman World Championship. The ascent to Hawi is long and plodding, and the belligerent winds along the way are as legendary as the climb itself. Deep, serpentine gorges formed by lava flow serve as conduits for violent wind bursts that threaten to send cyclists sprawling. And then there is the sun. It is inescapable. It beats down on the black lava rock and pavement before being radiated back up by the same, creating a vortex of heat that is almost unbearable by the time the sun fully crests the sky. Having sacrificed their quads in formal excise, athletes are treated to an inspiriting but painfully brief twelve-mile descent back down the Queen K. It is a momentary respite. Another fifty miles of stark terrain and gale force winds lie ahead.

The first surge of panic I felt came just over one hundred miles into the bike. It was strange timing for fear to make an appearance. Only a few miles of the bike leg remained, a relatively insignificant slab of pavement when you consider the total distance of the race. Up to this point, I had felt strong and confident. The swim had gone well. I had climbed out of the water a few minutes slower than I had hoped, but I had taken my time and, most importantly, I had avoided any unsolicited pummeling. I even gained some ground during the sixty-five-mile trip to the top of Hawi; by mile eighty, I started passing people for the first time.

The burst of energy came as if on cue. At mile eighty-five, I saw part of my army standing in formation along the side of the highway. They were easy to spot; the Team Teri T-shirts with their arresting bright blue swirl pattern popped against the pavement. They had made the excursion to Waikoloa in anticipation of catching me on my descent from Hawi and passed the time waiting by doing the wave as cyclists whooshed past, one after another. Several hours later, I arrived.

"Is that Teri . . .? Hey! Guys! I think that's Teri!"

"There she is!"

"Here she comes . . . Teri! Teri! Yay! Teri!"

Dave, Kyle, and Kati, along with Dave's brothers and their wives, cheered and clapped as I pulled over to the side of the road. I unclipped my feet from the pedals and hugged them.

"I was afraid I wouldn't see you guys!" I cried as I kissed Dave. "How long have you been here? Are you bored?"

"Teri, you look great! How do you feel?"

"You look really strong!"

"I feel great! Really. It's good! Not too windy."

Yes, I felt good. Then. But something had happened between the time I clipped back into my pedals and the sudden onset of alarm at mile one hundred.

Most likely, the interim twenty miles had happened.

Hours of biking on the Queen K were beginning to take their toll. Fatigue washed over me with devastating enormity. Jeff's nutrition notes remained neglected in the plastic armband around my wrist. I didn't feel terribly nauseated; I just wasn't hungry. At all. The thought of trying to consume a Cliff Bar or—heaven forbid—another GU packet, was enough to make my stomach revolt. I swallowed a few bites of the occasional banana I picked up at the aid stations, but overall, my caloric intake was insufficient. Jeff wouldn't have been pleased.

Feeling my emotions begin to crumble, I began singing. U2. "Beautiful Day." The anthem repeated itself in my head, over and over again.

Only a few more miles to go, I reminded myself. *Only a few more miles to go. And it is such a beautiful day . . .*

A full marathon awaited me still, but the run had no place in my mind at that moment. I avoided thinking too far ahead. Mental discipline is vital in endurance sport. And in cancer.

It's a beautiful day . . . Sky falls . . . it feels like it's a beautiful day . . . Don't let it get away . . .

The sun stilled burned with late afternoon intensity by the time I emerged from the transition area for the second time and began the run. Dusk was on its way, but it hadn't arrived yet. My army stationed themselves at the "Hot Corner," the bustling interchange at Palani Road and Ali'i Drive where miles one, ten, and twenty-five of the marathon converge. The three lanes run parallel to each other and are divided by triangular flags strung across the top of bright orange pylons. The first lane leads from the transition area and into the first miles of the marathon course. The outside lane is mile ten, steering participants up Palani, the soul-crushing hill that bludgeons legs already punished by the swim and bike. And sandwiched between the excited solemnity of those just beginning the run and the pensive preparation of those about to tackle the ascent of Palani is mile twenty-five, the final steps of the 140.6-mile journey.

Within this single stretch of pavement flanked by flapping banners and walls of spectators, the story of the Ironman unfolds. It is written on the faces of the athletes filing past—sprinting, walking, jogging, shuffling, limping, staggering, smiling, groaning, gasping, eyes filled with tears and eyes barely open. It is a poignant chronology narrated in three-part harmony. It is two thousand stories assembled in a single, volatile intersection. The Hot Corner is a charged one.

I saw my army the moment I set foot on Ali'i Drive. I cut across the road, making a quick detour to kiss Dave and greet the rest of the crew. Seeing my family and friends along the course provided immeasurable encouragement. Their hugs and kisses fortified me, getting me from one point to the next, like David describes in the Psalms, going from "strength to strength." I'd see the bright patch of blue swirl Team Teri shirts among the crowds and immediately feel revived.

Being a spectator at Kona is an endurance test in itself, demanding navigational skills, strategy, and the desire to lose your voice cheering. After all, a seventeen-hour race sprawled across 140.6 miles generally isn't considered an ideal spectator event. Closed roads, inaccessible terrain, and highways-turned-parking lots make timely navigation difficult, and you must sketch careful blueprints in order to catch a glimpse of your athlete. It is but a momentary sighting. You have just enough time to verbalize several frantic, impassioned salutes ("You look great!" "So strong!" "Keep going!") before she disappears. And then you wait, hour after hour, for a few precious seconds to see her again. For many family and friends, it is a twenty-hour day, beginning at 4:00 a.m. (spectators begin claiming their territory at Kailua Pier three hours before the swim start) and ending only when the last competitor crosses the finish line at midnight.

For their part, my army fashioned an elaborate and coordinated cheer system, facilitated by a massive exchange of cell phone numbers, island maps, modes of transportation (from SUVs to cars to bikes), and designated cheer spots. After the swim, they dispersed across the island, adventuring to specified locations and relaying updates after I passed. Then each group would pack up and move on to the next spot, repeating the process of waiting, cheering, and updating. We knew the bright blue shirts would make the army easier to spot—for me and for the soldiers themselves—but what we didn't expect was the response the shirts would prompt from other spectators along the course. Noticing the packs of "Team Teri: Powered By Hope" troops navigating the island, people asked questions. What do the shirts mean? Who is Teri? Are the shirts for sale? By the end of the day, hundreds upon hundreds of people knew my story, and when I would run by my family and friends, not only would my army cheer, but so would scores of spectators around them.

Now, just beginning the marathon, I assured my army that I was feeling strong. I knew their worry was increasing as the race progressed, and I wanted to give them as much confidence as I could before heading off for the ten-mile out-and-back before Palani. While I ran, the army headed down Ali'i Drive to find a place to eat. They had just enough time for a meal before trekking back to the Hot Corner to cheer me up the notorious climb. Palani would be my last chance to see them before the finish line.

It isn't until the run that you notice how much time has passed. The sun sets and begins to cast its long, solemn shadows across the streets speckled with solitary pilgrims. They travel by foot now, single-minded in purpose, unwavering in resolve. Only as you watch their bodies disappear into an ever-darkening road do you realize the day has aged. The sun has grown old in its long journey across the sky, and the deity that once clambered up the summit of the heavens defers to the night and sinks slowly beyond the horizon. A singular serenity settles over the Hot Corner as light gives way to dark. The garish wind and heat of Hawi seems but a distant memory. Occasionally, participants cross paths—those finishing the race with a great, final push and those with sixteen miles yet to go. It is heartbreaking and inspiring.

Miles past the wayfaring shadows of Palani, I made my way through the Energy Lab, an infamous six-mile stretch of pavement lined with giant solar panels. Named for the actual natural energy lab flanking its sides, it is both literal and sardonic in nature. During the day, it is a source of power that intensifies the already scathing heat, draining the life from itinerant triathletes. At night, it swallows any glimmer of light in an inky grave. I was barely able to see more than a few feet in front of me. Aid stations were situated at one-mile intervals, the only source of light. Long gone was the companionship of other runners; the miles had plunked great gaps between us and the dark had erased those within striking range. I knew if I could only make it through the Energy Lab, I would finish the race. I could hear the ocean lapping against the shore. I hadn't realized it was so close.

At some point during the run, I decided to fill my hat with ice at every aid station. It was a good decision, one that helped regulate my body temperature despite sauna-like conditions. Plus, it gave me something to look forward to. I sang and prayed as I ran. I recited the serenity prayer. I talked to my Grandma Ida and my dad. I thanked them for all they had done for me, for everything they taught me. I asked them to help me be strong.

"Give thanks to the Lord, for He is good! His love endures forever!"

I couldn't see the road ahead. But I didn't need to. My job wasn't to know the future—not in life, not with cancer, not here in the Energy Lab. My job was simply to take the next step, regardless of fears, fatigue, and previous failings. Grace demanded it.

"From the rising to the setting sun—His love endures forever! By the grace of God we will carry on—His love endures forever!"

Based on Psalm 136, the song speaks of God's miracles and faithfulness to the Israelites in the midst of impossible circumstances. It is the words of David put to music. It is one of my favorite songs. Though it was too dark to see the number marked on my arm and the bib number pinned to my shorts, I knew. 136. My race number was 136.

I don't believe in coincidences.

Fourteen hours into the race, I began to wonder about the finish line. I could hear it now, the thumping bass and the cheering crowd. It sounded like a party. It was a party. I knew my family and army were there, waiting for me. I wondered what I would do when I crossed the finish line. Stay cool? Do something with a bit more . . . pizzazz? I figured I'd do the latter, though I left the specifics to the spontaneity of the moment. Maybe I'd jump up and down. Maybe I'd dance. Get funky even.

As it turned out, my plans didn't matter. Just as I entered the finish chute, I saw Christi, Cary, Courtney, and Wilson. The wellspring of emotion dammed up over the course of the race burst forth. My family was crying. I was crying. In fact, everyone within a twenty-foot radius was crying. My great-nieces had shared my story with the spectators around them. Now total strangers cheered and cried as friends. With deep sobs, I embraced my family.

And then, once more, I began running.

I ran past the raised hands and pumped fists and uplifted signs. I ran past the clanging cowbells and banging sticks and whirling noisemakers. I ran past the towering succession of palm trees and international flags waving above an equally international crowd. I ran past the giant white fence panels, wholly sponsored yet strangely noncommercial. I even ran past the NBC cameras and lights as they filmed the final yards of the race.

And somehow, in the midst of the jubilation and floodlights and music and cheers—time stopped. Cancer fell away. Chemo fell away. The darkest moments of addiction and rehab, the devastation of my diagnosis, the painful conversations with my family, the long days in the hospital, the tears, the anger, the fear, the uncertainty—everything fell away.

Waiting for me just on the other side of the finish line was my family: Dave, Kyle, Kati, my mom, JoAnn, Mimi and, of course, Dr. Tan. They were smiling and clapping and crying. After fourteen hours on the course; fourteen hours in the sun, in the heat, and beneath the stars; fourteen hours since I treaded water in Kailua Bay and waved to Dave and Kyle and Kati, I saw them once more. The faces of those who mean more to me than anything in this world. They were with me at the start. They were with me now, at the finish. They had been with me the whole way.

My army couldn't jump in the water for me or pedal my bike while I caught my breath or take my place for a few miles on the run. No one could bring me closer to the finish line or make my race shorter. No one could take the cancer from my life. Ultimately, the journey was mine, and I alone was responsible for taking the next step. But they could walk with me along the way.

And they had.

This—all of this—was extraordinary. I didn't know what the days ahead would hold—if I had months left or if I had years, if I would see my children get married or if I would ever meet my grandchildren, if I would grow old with Dave or know a time once more when cancer wasn't a part of my life. The only thing I knew was that, no matter what, I was not alone. Not in my trials. Not in my triumphs.

I hadn't expected this—any of it. Not the depth of my struggles. Not the intensity of my joy. But God had given me a platform for victory. And this, this race, was my manifesto of hope.

I threw my hands in the air as I crossed the finish line. It was a declaration of faith. It was a celebration of grace. I was not alone. Everyone has a cancer, and everyone has a dream.

This just happened to be mine.

14

HOPE MARCHES ON

—————————

Races are funny things. In the midst of them, nothing else matters. When they are over, you move on. The world doesn't stop. The sun still rises and sets. The days still press forward. Life continues. But you are not the same for having endured. You cannot be.

Hours after we returned home from Hawaii, I headed back to Siteman and all of its waiting rooms, weigh stations, examination tables, and treatment chairs. The nurses hooked me up to the IV, the chemo started pumping in, and I was a cancer patient once more.

It was hard to imagine that the body sitting in the sterile confines of a hospital, tethered to beeping machines and bags of medicine, was just days before racing with some of the world's most elite athletes. With the memory of Kona so close, and my tan lines from the race still sharp and visible, I felt almost silly sitting in the treatment chair. I felt like I embodied such a strange dichotomy. On one hand, I was terrifically fit. On the other, I was very, very ill. It was unexpected. It was difficult to comprehend. It was really rather extraordinary.

When I was diagnosed with stage IV colon cancer, I didn't think it would evolve into an opportunity to inspire thousands of people or save hundreds of lives. I never saw my situation or myself in that light. I knew only that cancer wasn't going to stop me from training, from racing, from living. I knew only that I wanted to keep doing what I loved to do. That I still wanted to live fully. And I knew that in order to do so, I needed to focus not on the uncertainty ahead, but on all that God had done for me in the past.

There is a verse in the old hymn "Amazing Grace" that resonates vividly with me:

Through many dangers, toils, and snares
I have already come;
'Tis Grace that brought me safe thus far
And Grace will lead me home.

By the simplest of descriptions, grace is unmerited favor and reward. It is the freewill giving of what we cannot attain on our own. Grace cannot be earned or achieved. It is the opposite of doing. It is being done unto. Grace isn't given because we are perfect; it is given precisely because we are not.

But a simple definition proves obscenely inadequate, for grace is not cheap, nor is it static. It is not to be pocketed and used later as a "Get Out of Jail Free" card. We are not to be the same for having received grace. Its beauty elicits a response, one prompted by a deep, startling understanding of the favored bestowed. Grace comes with both opportunity and responsibility.

For me, grace was a new beginning. Reaching down into the recesses of addiction, grace was an unexpected emancipator, freeing me from my fears and insecurities. Grace let me know that I was okay, giving me an inner peace that transcended both fleeting emotions and deep struggles. I had seen the insidious futility of spiritual autonomy. I had experienced the devastating cycle of guilt and shame. But once I received full, undeserved forgiveness from the Highest Authority, I was overwhelmed with gratitude for what I had been given. Action was the overflow of that gratitude. And grace, far from being a one-and-done commodity, proved itself to be a great adventure.

Many people are amazed by how I've dealt with cancer physically. They ask if I was tired during the race, if I felt sick, if my legs hurt, if I ever wanted to quit. They ask me how I can continue to train and race while undergoing cancer treatment. The answer is I don't know. Maybe my body does hurt but I block it out. Maybe I have a high tolerance for pain. Maybe it's a bit of both. What I do know is that gratitude places a barrier between you and your pain. I make a conscious effort to focus on all the things with which I have been blessed—from my family to the incredible support crew around me to the simple ability to get up and go for a run. I am deliberate in not giving negative emotions the light of day. I don't go there. I can't. If I did, I wouldn't be able to do what I've been doing.

Looking back, I see God was preparing me for this experience with cancer. I don't believe anything happens by coincidence. This whole experience of merging Ironman training and cancer was spiritual and emotional more than anything else. The physical was simply the outward manifestation of an inner revolution. I don't feel that I'm mentally stronger than anyone else—I don't even know that I'm mentally stronger than I was years ago. And I am by no means perfect. There are still times when fear and doubt will creep in. I don't know what next year will bring. I don't know if there will be a next year. But my purpose has changed. My purpose is stronger than it was before. To this day I believe that God had me seek and look for a deeper purpose in my spiritual life before this whole experience with cancer. He wanted me to be prepared to have faith and trust and confidence that He would carry me through this. He wanted me to be prepared to accept a new, greater ambition. I know there is a bigger purpose to this whole story—one yet to be revealed, one beyond my own vision and ability. And every day I pray and actively seek how I can fulfill that purpose.

When I see people going through a hard time— myself included—I want to tell them never to give up. Because anything really is possible, whether it be a miracle, a cure, or an option we can't even imagine. No matter what our struggles are, we can all live full lives. We can use our cancer, whatever it may be, as a platform for victory. We can decide not to let our cancer define us. We can decide not to let our cancer dictate our lives. We can decide to take charge and embark on a great adventure and inspire others along the way. For true inspiration comes through living and leading by example. It's not about the big things. It's about the small decisions we make every day. To embrace challenges. To tackle the unknown. To forgive ourselves. To forgive others. To choose adventure even when we are scared. To persevere even when it is very, very hard. To always move forward. Because extraordinary arises from ordinary situations, and the decisions we make when no one is looking determine what others see when we are thrown under the spotlight. Because we can be diagnosed or we can be commissioned.

The choice is up to us.

After completing the Ironman World Championship in Kona, Teri went on to achieve her goal of racing all six world marathon majors in New York, Boston, Chicago, London, Berlin, and Tokyo. In 2013, she competed in the 70.3 Ironman World Championship in Las Vegas. Teri continues to battle cancer and receive maintenance chemo.

She has no plans to stop training.